THE JOY OF
Cookies

SHARON TYLER HERBST

New York • London • Toronto • Sydney

All inquiries should be addressed to
Barron's Educational Series, Inc.
250 Wireless Boulevard
Hauppauge, New York 11788

**Library of Congress
Cataloging-in-Publication Data**

Herbst, Sharon Tyler.
    The joy of cookies.
    Includes index.
    1. Cookies. I. Title.
TX772.H47
1987   641.8'654   87-1755
ISBN 0-8120-4518-1 (pbk)
ISBN 0-8120-5839-9

**PRINTED IN THE UNITED STATES OF
AMERICA**
0123 9770 98765432

*Dedicated, with love, to my husband Ron,
without whom there would be no joy . . .
and, quite literally, no* Joy of Cookies!

Special thanks to . . .

- *my mother and father, Kay and Wayne Tyler, and my sister, Tia Leslie, for their unstinting love and support. Extra thanks, Mom, for digging through all your heritage cookie recipes for me, and Dad, for being so brave about tasting so many testings!*

- *Bert Greene, for, his sage advice, for always encouraging me to reach for greater heights, and for being such a dear friend.*

Credits

Cover and book design: Milton Glaser, Inc.
Color photographs: Matthew Klein
Food styling: Andrea Swenson
Photo styling: Linda Cheverton

Recipes on pages 114, 124 and 140 have been adapted and reprinted from the author's book, *Simply Sensational Desserts*, published by HPBooks.

Photo Credits

Kentucky Bourbon Bars: Porcelain plates, cup and saucer by Cerelaine at Baccarat, New York. Silver spoon by Christofle at Baccarat, New York.
Old-Fashioned Brown Sugar Drops: Porcelain dessert plate by Cerelaine at Baccarat, New York
Double-Fudge Brownies: Porcelain dessert plate by Royal Copenhagen, New York. Dessert spoon by Christofle at Baccarat, New York.

Cherry Sweethearts: Porcelain plate by Cerelaine at Baccarat, New York
Moravian Molasses Cookies: Plate and mug from Royal Copenhagen, New York
Danish Dandies: Porcelain dessert service from Royal Copenhagen, New York. Silver demi-tasse spoon by Christofle at Baccarat, New York
"Stained Glass" Christmas Cookies: Silver tray by Ercuis at Baccarat, New York

Table of Contents

Foreword

by Bert Greene

Say "cookie?" to a small child (or a middle-aged man for that matter) and for your efforts you will receive (a) an instant sigh of pleasure followed by (b) an outstretched palm. A petition I have learned over the years: to reward at once with something sweet and crunchy *or* take the consequences. For nothing in the culinary lexicon with the exception of vanilla ice cream elicits such an immediate response or such an audible demand as a cookie. Whether the question is posed in English, French, Greek, German, or Swahili!

Speaking of cookies' universal appeal brings me to the heart of this book. For years I have been hoping someone would come along and compile a really first-rate baking *baedeker* that would define, and more importantly, demystify the concoction of all the sweet and sensuous cookies of the world. A recipe book of easy-to-acquire ingredients and fail-safe instruction that could with any luck turn a tot or a totterer at the stove into an instant Escoffier. Lo and behold, Sharon Tyler Herbst has done just that. Tying on her prettiest apron, flouring her cookie cutters and buttering her pans, she has addressed the task of cookie making with common sense, clarity and supreme confidence and expertise that communicates itself in every one of the recipes that follow. Forgive the pun, if I say that her "Joy of Cookies" is actually a piece of cake!

Introduction

Cookies . . . The International "Comfort Food"
Whether the cookie jar is half full or half
empty depends on whether one asks the
cookie baker or the cookie muncher!

*H*aving been born at noon on Thanksgiving day, I've always had a natural—even passionate—affinity for food . . . a seemingly logical predilection for one arriving on America's national day of feasting. By the same token, autumn is one of my favorite times of year because it always signals the start of earnest cookie baking. When I was a little girl growing up in Denver, my sister Tia and I knew that when our breath smoked the windowpane it was time to put Mom on a "cookie alert." The first day of autumn baking was a heady experience, with the day outside frosty and crisp, and inside the house all aglow with the warmth and fragrance of cookies baking. I used to think it was little-girl heaven . . . now I know such experiences are for all who are young at heart.

Though the word "cookie" is derived from the Dutch *koekje* ("little cake"), the earliest cookie-style cakes are thought to date back to 7th-century Persia, one of the first countries to cultivate sugar. A cookie by any other name is not necessarily "cookie." In England, cookies are called *biscuits*, in Spain they're *galletas*, Germans call them *keks*, Italians have their *biscotti*, and so it goes. *The Joy of Cookies* brings you a collection of over 200 favorite cookie recipes from around the world—many of them centuries old! Over 50 nations are deliciously represented in the following pages. I've made every effort to retain each heritage cookie's original character while adapting the recipes to use modern measurements and baking techniques. In many cases, the cookie's foreign name and origin are included for those who wish a touch of ethnic authenticity.

One theme that threads throughout the history of cookies is the important role they've always played in festive celebrations—from christenings and weddings to Easter and Christmas. Whatever the occasion, cookies' universal appeal undoubtedly comes from their extraordinary diversity. They can be crisp and dainty, big and chewy, filled, frosted . . . you name it! Cookie baking is creative, delivers almost immediate gratification and isn't at all intimidating.

Each country has several favorite traditional cookies. More often than not, they're made with some of the land's most basic and bountiful foods. For instance, oats are popular in Scottish cookies because, with Scotland's climate inhospitable to wheat growing, oats have taken over as a major crop. Likewise, because the date palm is prolific in North Africa and many Middle Eastern countries, dates are a common ingredient in cookies from those areas.

There's something magic about the fragrance of warm, freshly baked cookies that sets mouths to watering and kindles treasured memories of days gone by. A homemade cookie can do more to quickly dry an eye and cheer the spirit than all the words in the world. Maybe it's because homemade cookies always say "love" . . . both in the baking and in the sharing of them with someone special.

Whether you like your cookies buttery-crisp, moistly soft, gooey, chewy, small, large, fancy, or simple, you're bound to find a favorite in the following pages. Some are quick and easy and can be made in a flash. Others, though not difficult, take more time but are worth the extra effort because the results are so spectacular. May you enjoy making them as much as everyone else will enjoy eating them. And remember, when you bake homemade cookies, you're sharing more than food . . . you're sharing yourself, and you're giving *The Joy of Cookies*!

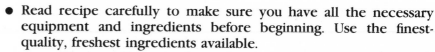

Cookie-Talk

Quick Tips for Cookie Success

Wooden Spoons

Pastry Blender

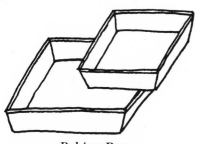

Baking Pans

- Read recipe carefully to make sure you have all the necessary equipment and ingredients before beginning. Use the finest-quality, freshest ingredients available.
- Assemble ingredients in the order they'll be used. For morning baking, assemble, measure, and cover ingredients the night before.
- Use the appropriate measuring cups—nested cups for dry ingredients, glass cups for liquids.
- Cracking eggs into a small bowl before adding them to other ingredients will prevent a spoiled egg or piece of shell from ruining the rest of the mixture.
- Making cookies the same size and shape will promote even baking and browning.
- Use vegetable shortening or unsalted butter or margarine to grease baking sheets. Salted butter or margarine may cause cookies to stick and overbrown.
- Set rack in middle of oven; preheat oven 10 to 15 minutes. Use an oven thermometer for accurate temperatures.
- If baking more than one sheet of cookies at a time, ensure even browning by rotating sheets from top to bottom and front to back halfway through baking time.
- Use a timer for accuracy. Prevent overbaking by checking cookies a couple of minutes before the minimum baking time.
- Let baking sheets cool, regreasing if necessary, between batches. Hot baking sheets will begin to melt the dough, creating changes in a cookie's texture and shape.
- As a rule, cookies should be removed quickly from baking sheets to prevent continued cooking. Refer to individual recipe.

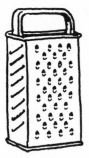

Box Grater

Pastry Brush

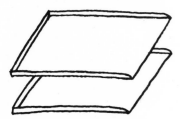

Baking Sheets

Cookie Dough Cutter

- Cool individual cookies on a rack to prevent soggy bottoms; cool bar cookies in pan on a rack.
- Store cooled cookies in airtight containers. Crisp and soft cookies must be stored separately to prevent the crisp ones from becoming soft.

Cookie Baking Basics

***P**reheating The Oven:* Turn the oven to the designated temperature 10 to 15 minutes before beginning to bake. Reduce the temperature by 25°F when using glass baking pans. Most cookies require a short baking time, so accurate temperatures are vital. A small investment in a good oven thermometer is valuable insurance against baking disasters. Mercury oven thermometers, available at kitchen supply shops, are best. The all-metal type found in supermarkets can become unreliable after a small jolt or fall.

Baking Sheets: Shiny heavy-gauge aluminum baking sheets are good heat conductors and will produce the most evenly baked and browned cookies. Dark sheets absorb too much oven heat and can overbrown (or burn) your cookies. This problem can be alleviated by lining them with heavy-duty aluminum foil. Insulated baking sheets (two sheets of aluminum with an air space sealed between them) are good for soft cookies but not for crisp ones, which won't get really crisp. Cookies may take a minute or so longer on insulated sheets. If you only have lightweight baking sheets, place one on top of the other to prevent cookies from burning. In a pinch, invert a jelly-roll pan and bake on the bottom. Unless a cookie dough requires refrigeration, baking sheets or pans should be prepared before the dough is mixed. Use shortening, unsalted butter or unsalted margarine to lightly coat baking sheets with a thin film of fat. Too much fat can cause cookies to spread and overbrown on the bottom. Use your fingers or a piece of crumpled paper towel to grease baking sheets. *To flour baking sheets*: Grease sheet, then

Measuring Spoons

Nested Measuring Cups

Liquid Measuring Cup

Rubber Spatula

sprinkle with about ½ tablespoon flour; tap and rotate sheet until entire surface is coated with flour. Turn sheet upside down over the sink and shake it gently to remove excess flour.

Measurements Make a Difference: Accurate measurements are more important in baking than in any other form of cookery.

Measuring Spoons come in nested sets ranging in size from ⅛ teaspoon to 1 tablespoon. Pour or scoop dry ingredients into spoon; level with the straight edge of a knife (not your finger!). Liquid ingredients should be poured into spoon until full.

Dry Measuring Cups come in nested sets which can include 2-cup, 1-cup, ½-cup, ⅓-cup, ¼-cup and ⅛-cup (2-tablespoon) sizes. To measure flour and powdered sugar, stir and lightly spoon into measuring cup; level with the straight edge of a knife. Do not tap or press flour into cup before measuring. Do not sift flour for recipes in this book; sift powdered sugar only if it is lumpy or the recipe so directs. To measure brown sugar, shortening and other fats, pack down firmly into cup; level with a knife. For coconut, nuts and chopped dried fruits, fill cup, then level with your fingers.

Liquid Measuring Cups range in size from 1 to 4 cups. To use, pour in liquid; read measurement at eye level.

Mixing Cookie Doughs: Beating the softened fat and sugar together, either by hand or electric mixer, is the first step in many cookie doughs. It's important for several reasons: to thoroughly combine the ingredients, to begin dissolving the sugar and to incorporate air into the dough. In most cases (depending on the ratio of sugar to fat), beating the mixture will cause it to become light in color and fluffy in texture. Eggs and other liquids are usually beaten into the mixture at this point. Flour and other dry ingredients are generally combined in a separate bowl, then stirred by hand into the butter mixture. Unless the recipe so directs, sifting the ingredients together is unnecessary. Once the flour is

Mortar and Pestle

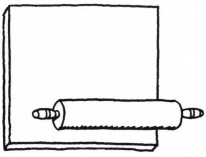

Pastry Board and Rolling Pin

Nut Chopper

added, care should be taken not to overmix the dough. Too much handling develops the gluten in the flour and can produce tough cookies. Extras, such as fruits, nuts, and chocolate chips, are usually stirred in.

Shaping the Dough: There are six basic cookie styles: *Drop Cookies* are made by dropping spoonfuls of dough onto cookie sheets. *Bar Cookies* are created when a batter or soft dough is spooned into a shallow pan, then baked, cooled and cut into bars. *Hand-Formed (or Molded) Cookies* are made by shaping dough by hand into balls, logs, crescents and other shapes. *Pressed Cookies* are formed by pressing dough through a cookie press (or pastry bag with a decorative tip) to form fancy shapes and designs. *Refrigerator Cookies* are made by shaping the dough into logs that are refrigerated until firm, then sliced and baked. *Rolled Cookies* begin by rolling the dough out into a thin layer, then cutting it into decorative shapes. The individual chapter introductions give details on each style of cookie.

Placing Cookie Dough on Baking Sheets: Use a metal spatula to transfer rolled cookie cutouts to baking sheets. Always place dough on a cool baking sheet; warm sheets will cause cookies to spread and flatten. To speed the baking process, line a baking sheet with foil, bake the cookies, then slip the cookie-covered foil off the sheet. Quickly cool the baking sheet to room temperature (stick it in the refrigerator for a couple of minutes). Slide the cooled baking sheet under another dough-covered piece of foil and bake.

Baking Cookies: Always begin baking in a preheated oven. Cookies will bake more evenly if only one sheet at a time is baked on the center oven rack. For even heat circulation, baking sheets should be at least 2 inches smaller all around than your oven. If you're baking 2 sheets of cookies at once, make sure the oven racks are spaced at least 6 inches apart. For more even baking, rotate the baking sheets front to back and top to bottom halfway through baking time.

Sieve (Strainer)

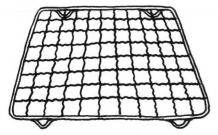

Wire Cooling Rack

Pastry Scraper

Sharp, Pointed Knife

Testing Cookies for Doneness: To allow for variance in individual ovens, always check for a cookie's doneness a few minutes before the minimum time listed in the recipe. A couple of minutes can make a big difference with cookies, and overbaked cookies are always disappointing. When checking for doneness, open and shut the door as quickly as possible to prevent excess loss of heat; an oven can lose up to a third of its heat in just a few seconds. If it's necessary to check the bottom of a cookie, or to use a toothpick to test a bar cookie, remove the cookies from the oven and leave the door closed while you test.

Cooling Cookies: Cookies are cooled on raised racks called— appropriately—cooling racks. A substitute can be made by setting a wire oven or refrigerator rack on 4 tuna cans. Most individual cookies are cooled directly on a rack, bar cookies in their pan on a rack. Immediately after baking, use a wide metal spatula to carefully transfer cookies from baking sheet to rack. Some recipes for soft or fragile cookies suggest that they stand on the baking sheet for a few minutes in order to become firm before being moved. If not removed from the baking sheet soon enough, certain cookies, such as the *Brazil Nut Wafers*, page *86*, may stick to the baking sheet. If that happens, simply return the cookies to the warm oven for a few seconds to loosen them.

Decorating Cookies: Decorations such as colored sugar, silver dragees, candy confetti, nuts and candied fruit can be applied before or after baking. To decorate before baking, brush surface of cookies with an egg glaze made by mixing one egg white with 2 teaspoons water; sprinkle with desired topping and bake. To decorate cookies after baking, frost or glaze the cooled cookies; immediately sprinkle with desired decoration before topping sets.

Cookie-Forming Tools

Cookie Cutters come in all sizes and shapes. Use sturdy, sharp-edged cutters as close as possible to the size recommended in the

Cookie Cutters

Wire Whisk

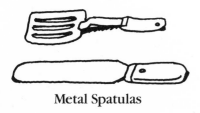

Metal Spatulas

recipe. Cut cookies close together; dip cutters that stick to the dough into flour or sugar. A *roller-cutter*—a metal or plastic cylinder marked with assorted designs—makes quick work of cutting out cookie dough. Just roll the cutter across the dough and *voilà*!—your cookies are cut.

Cookie Molds and Carved Rolling Pins are used to create designs in some European cookies. Wooden molds, available in specialty shops, come in all sizes and shapes. The dough is pressed into a floured mold and leveled off. The mold is then inverted and tapped sharply on the back to release the molded cookie. Special carved rolling pins imprint designs when rolled across and pressed into a sheet of dough (see *Springerle*, page *186*). The dough is then cut apart to form individual cookies.

Cookie Presses (also called cookie "guns") are used to make spritz and other pressed cookies. They come with a selection of templates in various designs. A soft dough is spooned into the press, then pushed through the template to form a design.

Cookie Stamps imprint a design on the dough's surface. A ridged or patterned meat tenderizing mallet will achieve similar results.

Pastry Bags, used for piping cookies onto baking sheets, are cone-shaped bags with a large opening at one end (for spooning in doughs) and a small opening at the other (for a decorative tip). They come in various sizes (the most all-purpose being 12 to 14 inches long) and most are made of parchment or easy-to-clean plastic-lined cotton or canvas. You can make your own out of waxed paper (see page *148*).

Hints for Storing and Freezing Cookies

*N*early any cookie is at its very best when fresh. A few basic guidelines, however, will help keep your cookies almost first-day-fresh so they'll be good to the very last crumb. Freezing can hold your cookies' flavor in suspended animation for several months. Cookies in the freezer are a cook's culinary security!

Successfully Storing Cookies

- Most unbaked cookie doughs can be refrigerated for up to 2 weeks; frozen up to 4 months. Thaw frozen dough in the refrigerator overnight before forming and baking.
- Storage time for baked cookies is indicated in each recipe. The cookie may last more or less time, depending on the storage conditions.
- Make sure cookies are *completely* cool before storing.
- Store all single cookies in airtight containers such as screw-top jars or sealed plastic bags. This prevents humidity from softening crisp cookies and air from drying soft cookies. Never store crisp and soft cookies in the same container, or the crisp ones will soon be soft.
- Bar cookies may be stored, tightly covered, in the pan in which they were baked.
- If cookies require refrigeration, cover them tightly to prevent absorption of other food odors.
- Soft cookies that are dry because of overbaking or age may be resoftened by adding one or two apple quarters to the storage container. Let stand a day or two before removing the fruit.
- Crisp cookies that have softened can be recrisped in a 300°F oven for 3 to 5 minutes; cool on a rack before serving.
- Separate layers of decorated, moist or sticky cookies with waxed paper.
- Don't store cookies where air can circulate (such as on plates or in boxes or paper bags) and expect them to stay fresh.

Frozen Assets

- Make sure cookies to be frozen are wrapped airtight, either in foil or in freezer-weight plastic bags; expel as much air as possible.

Rigid plastic freezer containers may also be used and are especially good for delicate cookies.

- Always label your storage containers with a piece of tape indicating name of cookie, quantity and date stored.
- Unfrosted cookies can be frozen from 4 to 6 months, depending on the temperature and conditions in the freezer. Place a sheet of waxed paper or plastic wrap between cookie layers. It's best to frost cookies after freezing and thawing, but frosted cookies can be frozen for up to 3 months with the "flash-freeze" method (see next hint).
- Flash-freezing can alleviate the problem of soft cookies crumpling when packaged for freezing. *To flash-freeze cookies*: Place a tray of uncovered cookies in freezer; freeze until hard. Quickly wrap, label and return to freezer.
- Defrosting cookies takes 10 to 15 minutes at room temperature.
- Freeze refrigerator cookie dough for baking at a future date by wrapping it in plastic wrap, then in foil or plastic bags. When ready to bake, remove dough from freezer, slice and bake. If dough is too hard to slice immediately, let stand at room temperature for 30 minutes.

Packing and Mailing Cookies

*S*ending a package of homemade cookies to someone far away is the warmest way to say you care. Make sure you select sturdy cookies that will keep well. Bar, drop, fruit-filled and some hand-molded cookies are usually the best travelers. Avoid cookies with frostings or pointed edges; fragile, thin cookies run the risk of becoming cookie crumbs by the time they reach their destination.

Always wrap soft and crisp cookies separately to preserve their textures. Use foil to wrap cookies in pairs (flat sides together) or in small stacks. Or layer the cookies in rigid containers such as pretty tins, plastic or cardboard boxes or coffee or shortening cans with plastic lids. Pack the cookies close together so they won't have room to move around and break during transit; separate layers with waxed paper or plastic wrap. If packing a variety of cookies in one container, place several of one kind in separate cupcake liners.

Shrink-wrapping large individual cookies or small stacks of cookies preserves their freshness and looks professional. To shrink-wrap cookies, preheat oven to 325°F. Line a baking sheet with 2 layers of paper towels; set aside. Wrap cookie stacks or large single cookies firmly in a good-quality plastic wrap (bargain brands will melt!). Cut away any excess plastic wrap that bunches up at the overlap. Place paper towel-lined baking sheet in the oven for 5 minutes. Remove from oven; arrange wrapped cookies, an inch apart, on hot baking sheet. Return sheet to oven, leaving the door open slightly so you can watch the cookies closely. The plastic wrap will shrink tightly around the cookie packages in just a few seconds. Cool on racks before packing.

If sending more than one kind of cookie in the same container, place the heaviest cookies on the bottom. Pad the top of the container with crumpled waxed paper to keep cookies from jostling and breaking. If desired, gift-wrap the container for special occasions (see *Creative Ideas For Gift-Wrapping Cookies*, page *12*). If the container isn't airtight, seal it in a plastic bag.

Check with your postmaster or shipper regarding packaging requirements and mailing deadlines (particularly during holiday rushes). For special occasions, send the package a couple of days before you think it's necessary to insure against shipping or mailing delays.

Pack the container of cookies in sturdy packing boxes with plenty of room for a cushion of filler (crumpled newspaper or other paper, styrofoam pellets or plastic bubble-wrap). Pad the bottom of the box with several inches of filler, add the container of cookies, then more filler around the sides and on top. If sending more than one container of cookies in the same box, use filler to pad well between containers.

Seal the box tightly with strapping or package-sealing tape; do not use string. Clearly print address and return address on package; cover with transparent tape to protect from adverse weather. Mark *"fragile"* on the box in several places. Send the package by first-class mail so your cookies will arrive as fresh as possible.

Creative Ideas for Gift Wrapping Cookies

*C*ookie gifts become extra-special when you wrap them with a festive flair. Here are just a few ideas on ways to package and present your cookies:

- It's a good idea to line your container with plastic wrap or foil. This prevents butter in the cookies from spotting the container or the paper or fabric lining it.
- Scout flea markets and garage sales throughout the year for interesting cookie containers such as unusual tins, carved wooden plates, colorful baskets, old-fashioned crocks, or decorative and uniquely shaped plates and bowls.
- Look in card or specialty shops for brightly colored bags, gift boxes, colored cellophane and yarn.
- Use ribbon or yarn to attach fun and useful tie-ons (cookie cutters, miniature whisks, kitchen magnets, a pastry brush, rubber spatulas, wooden spoons, a bundle of cinnamon sticks, cookie stamps, measuring spoons, etc.) to your package.
- Line an attractive basket with a paper or cloth napkin, kitchen towel or colorful tissue wrapping paper.
- Place Easter cookies in a gaily colored basket filled with Easter grass.
- Use decorative, self-adhesive labels (available at gourmet and card shops) on which you can print the name of the cookie.

Opposite: Butterscotch-Chocolate Chip Chews (page 30).
Page following: Edinburgh Squares (page 34).

- Line brightly colored flower pots or planters with tissue wrapping paper; attach a miniature trowel to the ribbon.
- Package cookies in or with the pans in which they would be baked: madeleines with a madeleine mold, shortbread in a shortbread mold and so on.
- Decorate coffee or shortening cans with wrapping paper, paint or decorative stick-ons.

Ingredients

*A*lways use the finest-quality, freshest ingredients available. Your cookies will only be as good as what goes into them!

FLOUR—Most of the recipes in this book call for *all-purpose flour*, which comes unbleached (my preference) and bleached; they can be used interchangeably. Don't substitute any of the specialty flours such as cake, self-rising or bread flour—the results won't be the same. *Whole wheat flour* is denser and coarser than all-purpose. Substituting more than half whole wheat flour for all-purpose flour will create a coarse, heavy cookie. *Semolina flour*, used for the *Pistachio Butter Rings*, is a granular, high-gluten flour made from durum wheat. It can be found in health food stores.

LEAVENINGS—Not all cookies require leavenings, but the two most commonly used are baking powder and baking soda. *Baking powder* (a mixture of baking soda, an acid such as cream of tartar and a moisture absorber such as cornstarch) is perishable and should be stored in a cool, dry place. Use double-acting baking powder, which releases its first burst of carbon dioxide gas bubbles when combined with moisture, and a second burst when it's exposed to heat. *Baking soda* is generally used with acid ingredients such as buttermilk or molasses. Some older cookie recipes use a combination of baking soda and cream of tartar. A substitution of ¼ teaspoon baking soda plus ½ teaspoon cream of tartar may be used for each teaspoon of baking powder.

FATS—Before writing this book, I was in the habit of using butter in most of my cookies. In my research, however, I found that many recipes use shortening or lard . . . with delicious results! The fact is, adding spices, chocolate, fruit and such often completely obscures butter's wonderful flavor. So I encourage you to try other fats . . . be skeptical of the popular snobbish attitude that "only butter will do." It's simply not true!

Butter used in the following recipes is the *unsalted* variety—both for its sweet, creamy flavor and for the control it gives the cook over added salt. If you substitute salted butter, decrease the amount of salt in the recipe by at least half. Regular stick butter—not whipped—is the form used. *Margarine* can be substituted for butter but is not generally recommended because it produces a softer cookie dough and different results. Because salt acts as a preservative, unsalted butter turns rancid quickly; wrap it airtight and store in the freezer.

Shortening refers to all-vegetable shortening. For best results, keep shortening at room temperature.

Lard, rendered from pork, is oilier than most other fats and creates short, flaky cookies and pastries. Leaf lard, from the fat around the kidneys, is considered the best. Fresh lard has a slightly nutty flavor; it should be stored in the refrigerator.

EGGS used in these cookie recipes are large, Grade AA; Grade A may also be used. Using the correct-size egg in baked goods is vital. Too small, and your cookie dough may be too dry; larger-than-called-for eggs can produce a wet dough. Cold eggs are much easier to separate than those at room temperature.

Egg yolks that are unbroken can be covered with cool water, sealed tightly and refrigerated for 2 to 3 days. To freeze yolks, add a small pinch of salt or scant ¼ teaspoon sugar (depending on their intended future use) for each yolk; lightly whisk to combine. Store in an airtight jar or small plastic bag; label container with the number of yolks and whether salt or sugar was added. Freeze up to 6 months. Thaw in refrigerator before using in custards, sauces or dressings.

Egg whites should be at room temperature in order to obtain maximum volume when beaten. To quickly warm cold egg whites, set the bowl holding them in a larger bowl of warm (not hot) water. Stir occasionally until whites are room temperature. Beat egg whites in a dry glass, stainless steel or copper bowl that is *completely* free of grease. Store leftover egg whites, tightly covered, in the refrigerator up to 4 days. To freeze, place one egg white in each section of an ice cube tray. Freeze until solid; turn egg-white cubes into a plastic bag. Seal tightly and freeze up to one year. Use in soufflés, mousses or meringues.

SWEETENERS—Sugars and other sweeteners add flavor and tenderness to cookies; they also aid in browning. Each sugar has a definite structural function in baking. A liquid sweetener such as honey or corn syrup can't be substituted for granular sugar without changing the cookie's texture . . . sometimes drastically! If you must substitute, use this formula: For every cup of granular sweetener, use ½ cup liquid sweetener and decrease other liquid in the recipe by ¼ cup. Before measuring liquid sweeteners, lightly oil the measuring cup. The sweetener will slip out easily, without clinging to the cup.

Granulated sugar in the following recipes means regular granulated sugar, not superfine.

Brown sugar comes in "light" or "dark," the latter flavored more strongly with molasses. Unless a recipe otherwise indicates, use light brown sugar; dark can be substituted for a more intense flavor. Brown sugar can be substituted for granulated sugar, cup for cup. To measure brown sugar, pack it firmly into the cup; level with the straight edge of a knife. Brown sugar packaged in plastic bags stays softer than it does in boxes. To soften dry, hard brown sugar, put it in a plastic bag with one or two apple wedges and seal tightly. It will soften in a day or two. Or place brown sugar and apple wedges in a microwave-proof bowl, cover with plastic wrap and microwave on LOW 1 to 2 minutes.

Powdered sugar, also known as confectioners' sugar, has a flourlike consistency and is much less sweet than granulated sugar. It's the counterpart of the European *icing sugar* and contains a small amount of cornstarch to keep it from lumping. It melts differently when heated and therefore should not be substituted for granulated sugar in baking.

Coarse decorating sugar (also referred to as sugar crystals) has granules about 4 times larger than those of regular granulated sugar. It's used for decorating and can be found in cake-decorating-supply and gourmet shops. Regular *colored sugars* are available in most supermarkets.

Vanilla sugar is most often used to decorate cookies. It can also be a cookie ingredient by using 1 tablespoon for each ¼ teaspoon vanilla extract, decreasing accordingly the total amount of sugar used. *To make vanilla sugar*: Combine a pound of sugar (granulated or powdered) with 2 vanilla beans in an airtight container; push the beans well down into the sugar. Cover and let stand at least a week before using. One bean will flavor repeated batches of sugar; replenish the sugar as you use it. Replace the vanilla beans every 6 months.

Honey used in the following recipes is a mild honey, such as orange blossom. Store honey at room temperature. Reliquefy crystallized honey by setting the jar in a pan of hot water; stir occasionally until the honey is once again smooth. Or put the opened jar of honey in a microwave and cook at 100% power 20 seconds, or until crystals melt.

Molasses in this book means light, unsulphured molasses. It has a distinctive bittersweet flavor and is not as sweet as most other sugars. For a lighter molasses flavor, substitute half dark corn syrup.

Corn syrup comes in light and dark. Like granulated sugar, light corn syrup has little flavor; dark corn syrup tastes faintly of molasses.

Maple syrup in this book means *pure* maple syrup, not pancake syrup which, more often than not, is corn syrup with artificial maple flavoring. Pure maple syrup is more expensive, but there's no comparison in flavor. Refrigerate opened pure maple syrup to inhibit the growth of mold.

Golden syrup—the most well known brand being "Lyle's"—is a special sweetener made from evaporated sugar cane juice. It has a rich, nutty flavor unmatched by other liquid sweeteners.

DAIRY PRODUCTS—The fat in dairy products helps tenderize baked goods. *Whipping cream* contains from 35 to 40% milkfat, whereas *half & half* (half milk and half light cream) contains 12 to 15%. *Sour cream* (18 to 20% milkfat), made by souring light cream, has a delicious, slightly tart flavor. *Cream cheese* must contain at least 33% milkfat. Don't expect your cookies to be as tender if you substitute low-fat cream cheese. Always soften cream cheese before using in a cookie dough. In a pinch, soften it quickly by placing the unwrapped cheese on a dish in the microwave oven at 50% power for 30 to 60 seconds.

CHOCOLATE AND COCOA—The four types of chocolate used in this book are unsweetened chocolate, semisweet chocolate (chips and 1-ounce squares), white chocolate and cocoa powder. Because they all contain different amounts of sugar and cocoa butter, they're not readily interchangeable. Store chocolate in a dry, cool (68° to 78°F) place. Warmer temperatures are likely to cause a grayish "bloom," created when cocoa butter separates and rises to the surface. This bloom doesn't harm a chocolate's flavor or baking qualities.

To melt chocolate: Place coarsely chopped chocolate in the top of a double boiler over *simmering* water. Remove from heat when chocolate is halfway melted; stir until smooth. Or place chocolate in a glass bowl in a microwave oven. Cook, uncovered, at 50% power for 1 minute for the first ounce of chocolate; add 20 seconds for each additional ounce. Various chocolates have different consistencies when melted: unsweetened chocolate becomes runny, whereas semisweet and sweet chocolates hold their shape until stirred.

The single most important caveat when working with chocolate is, once it's melted, not to let any moisture come in contact with it. A few drops of water will cause chocolate to seize (clump and harden) into a stiff, unwieldy mass. Strangely enough, this problem can be rectified by adding ½ teaspoon more liquid (water, milk, vegetable oil, etc.) for each ounce of seized chocolate. Quickly stir liquid into chocolate; stir until smooth.

Unsweetened chocolate is bitter baker's chocolate unadulterated by any sweetener. Three tablespoons unsweetened cocoa powder plus 1 tablespoon butter can be substituted for 1 ounce of unsweetened chocolate.

Semisweet chocolate is sugar-sweetened bitter chocolate with extra cocoa butter for added smoothness. It's sold in 1-ounce squares, 6- to 16-ounce bars, chips/bits/morsels (standard or miniature) and a newer size, "chunks." When buying chocolate *chips* and *chunks*, be sure the label says "real chocolate," not "chocolate-flavored." The latter tastes like the impostor it is.

White chocolate is not really chocolate because it doesn't contain chocolate liquor, the thick, dark paste left after the cocoa butter is extracted from the nibs. White chocolate is very sweet and has just a whisper of chocolate flavor, contributed by the cocoa butter. It can be purchased in bulk at candy stores and gourmet shops and is now sold in chip form in many supermarkets. Be sure you buy "white chocolate" chips. Some look-alike chips are, in fact, vanilla-flavored. *Cocoa* refers to unsweetened cocoa powder, not sweetened cocoa mixes. I prefer Dutch-process cocoa, which has been treated with a small amount of alkali to produce a darker, less bitter product. Because cocoa is sometimes lumpy (and once moisture touches it the lumps remain), all of the following recipes advise mixing it either with sugar or flour before adding any liquid.

NUTS—Nuts should be very fresh; old or rancid nuts will spoil the flavor of your cookies. Store shelled and unshelled nuts in airtight containers in the freezer for 6 to 8 months.

Chopped nuts, as a phrase, can mean something different to each reader. The definitions used in this book for chopped and ground nuts (and the sizes they describe) are:

● *Coarsely chopped*—about the size of a dried navy bean.
● *Chopped*—the size of a raisin.
● *Finely chopped*—the size of currants or dried split peas.
● *Coarsely ground*—the consistency of coarse cornmeal.
● *Finely ground*—the consistency of granulated sugar.

Nuts can be chopped by hand, using a large French knife, or in the food processor with a metal blade. For maximum control with the food processor, chop only a cup or so at a time, using quick on/off pulses. The food processor also makes quick work of grinding nuts. Just make sure you watch them carefully, or you'll end up with nut butter!

Blanching nuts means removing the skins. *To blanch almonds*, cover them with an inch of boiling water; let stand 1 to 2 minutes before draining. Pop them out of their skins by squeezing between fingers and thumb. Dry and recrisp almonds by baking in a single layer at 175°F, stirring occasionally, for 30 minutes. *To blanch hazelnuts*, bake in a single layer at 350°F for 10 to 15 minutes or until the skins begin to flake. Place a handful at a time in a dish towel; fold the towel over the warm nuts and rub vigorously. Most of the skins will flake off; don't worry about stubborn bits that cling.

Toasting nuts, seeds (such as sesame) and oats intensifies their flavor. *Stovetop method*: Stirring frequently, cook nuts in an ungreased skillet over medium heat until golden brown. *Conventional oven method*: Place a single layer of nuts in a jelly-roll pan. Oven-toast at 350°F, stirring occasionally, 15 minutes, or until golden brown. *Microwave oven method*: Place nuts in a single layer on a paper or other microwave-proof plate; do not cover. Cook at 100% power, stirring once or twice, for 1 to 4 minutes, or until the nuts are pale golden.

FRUIT (Raisins, Currants, Coconut, Dried and Candied Fruits)

Dried Fruit that is purchased from a health food store or specialty shop will generally be much fresher and softer than that found in supermarkets. Store dried fruits in an airtight container in a cool place. "Dried-out" dried fruit can be rehydrated by covering it with boiling water and letting it stand for 10 minutes before draining.

Candied Fruit that magically materializes in supermarkets during the holidays is usually ages old and should be avoided. Specialty shops carry fresh candied fruits that will make your cookies irresistible. When chopping dried or candied fruit, keep it from sticking to the knife blade by first tossing it with a little of the flour or sugar called for in the recipe. Be sure to deduct the amount of flour or sugar used from the recipe. Store candied fruit at room temperature in airtight containers.

Coconut imparts a deliciously moist chewiness to cookies. Most of the recipes in this book use sweetened coconut—flaked or shredded—which can easily be found in any supermarket. Unsweetened coconut, sold in health food and specialty stores, and grated fresh coconut can be substituted; the cookie, of course, will not be as sweet. *Orange, Lemon and Lime Zest* is the colored portion of the citrus skin. Please don't cut corners by using bottled dried lemon or orange peel. It's virtually tasteless and bears no resemblance to the fragrant flavor of freshly grated zest!

OATMEAL AND GRANOLA—These cereals add texture and chewiness to cookies. Regular or quick-cooking (not instant) oatmeal and plain granola (without added fruits or nuts) were used for the recipes in this book.

SPICES—Because spices quickly lose their flavor and fragrance, it's best to buy them in small quantities. Store them in airtight containers away from heat and light. Old spices that have lost their "zip" will add little flavor—you might as well throw them out.

OTHER FLAVORINGS—Whenever possible, use pure (not imitation) extracts. This is especially important for *vanilla extract* which, in its pure form, delivers an unforgettable fragrance and flavor. Imitation vanilla flavoring, however, nas an insipid taste that is entirely forgettable. *Rosewater* is a distillation of rose petals, as *orange-flower water* is of bitter orange blossoms. They impart an elusive floral fragrance that permeates baked goods with exotic flavor. Both can be found in liquor stores, Middle Eastern markets and the gourmet section of most supermarkets.

Instant coffee powder adds color and flavor to baked goods. Instant coffee granules won't dissolve as readily as powder in most cookie mixtures. Make instant coffee *powder* from freeze-dried coffee granules by crushing them with a mortar and pestle or in a small bowl with the back of a spoon. For the deepest coffee flavor, use instant espresso powder. Potent potables such as *liquors, wines, and liqueurs* add flavor intrigue. Teetotalers needn't worry because the alcohol evaporates during the baking process, leaving only the liquor's delightful essence in the cookie.

What Went Wrong?

Problem	Cause	Solution
Cookie dough is dry and crumbly.	● Too much flour.	● Measure flour accurately. Do not pack flour into measure. Spoon it into measuring cup, then level with the straight edge of a knife.
	● Too little liquid or shortening.	● It's very important to use the correct size egg. Use large eggs for the following recipes; small or medium eggs won't provide enough liquid. Add 1 to 2 tablespoons milk or softened butter to dry dough. Butter will create a crisper cookie.
Cookie dough is too soft to hand-shape or roll; pressed cookie dough will not hold its design.	● Dough is too warm.	● Refrigerate dough until it becomes firm enough to handle. Work with small portions of dough at a time, leaving the rest refrigerated.
Cookies bake unevenly — some cookies are done before others.	● Dough was not uniformly shaped.	● Try to form cookies as close to the same size and shape as possible.
	● Hot spots in oven.	● Reverse baking sheet from front to back halfway through baking time. If using more than one baking sheet at a time, also rotate sheets from top to bottom.
Sides of baked cookies stick to each other.	● Cookies were placed too close together on baking sheet.	● Space cookies according to recipe directions — in general, 1 to 2 inches apart. Large drop cookies will usually require at least 2 inches between them. Use a knife or the edge of a metal spatula to cut stuck-together cookies apart before removing from baking sheets.

Problem	Cause	Solution
Cookies spread and flatten excessively on baking sheet.	• Baking sheet was overgreased.	• Use a thin, even layer of shortening or unsalted butter or margarine to grease baking sheets.
	• Cookie dough was placed on a hot baking sheet.	• Always cool baking sheets between batches. Stick the sheet in the refrigerator a few minutes for a quick cool-down.
Cookies stick to baking sheet.	• Baking sheet was not greased adequately or evenly.	• Make sure the shortening covers the baking sheet completely in an even layer.
	• Cookies remained on baking sheet too long after removing from oven.	• Return cookies to oven for a few seconds; remove immediately from baking sheets.
Cookies are too dark on the bottom.	• Baking sheet too thin or too dark.	• Use shiny heavy-gauge aluminum baking sheets. Or insulate a lightweight baking sheet by lining it with aluminum foil or a second baking sheet.
	• Cookies were baked on the lower oven shelf.	• For even browning, bake on middle oven shelf.
	• Baking sheets were overgreased.	• Use a thin, even layer of shortening or unsalted butter or margarine to grease baking sheets.
Cookies are too dry or too moist.	• Overbaking or underbaking.	• To prevent overbaking, always check cookies a few minutes before the minimum time indicated in recipe. Use an oven thermometer for accurate oven temperatures. Bake underdone cookies a few minutes longer, checking at 1- to 2-minute intervals.
Cookies crumble as they're removed from the baking sheet.	• Some butter-rich or soft cookies are quite fragile when hot.	• Allow cookies to cool on baking sheets 1 to 2 minutes before removing to a rack to cool.

Conversion Tables

The following are conversion tables and other informational items applicable to those converting recipes in this book for use in other English-speaking countries. The cup and spoon measures given in this book are U.S. Customary; use these tables when working with British Imperial or metric kitchen utensils.

Liquid Measures

The old Imperial pint is larger than the U.S. pint; therefore note the following when measuring liquid ingredients:

U.S.

1 cup = 8 fluid ounces
½ cup = 4 fluid ounces
1 tablespoon = ½ fluid ounce

Imperial

1 cup = 10 fluid ounces
½ cup = 5 fluid ounces
1 tablespoon = 1 fluid ounce

U.S. Measure	Metric	Imperial*
1 quart (4 cups)	946 ml	1½ pints + 4 tablespoons
1 pint (2 cups)	473 ml	¾ pint
1 cup	236 ml	¼ pint + 6 tablespoons
1 tablespoon	15 ml	1 ample tablespoon
1 teaspoon	5 ml	1 teaspoon

*Note that exact quantities cannot always be given. Differences are more crucial when dealing with larger quantities. For teaspoon and tablespoon measures, simply use scant quantities, or for more accurate conversions rely upon metric measures.

Oven Temperatures					
Gas Mark	¼	2	4	6	8
Fahrenheit	225°	300°	350°	400°	450°
Centigrade	107°	150°	178°	205°	233°

Weight and Volume Measures

U.S. cooking procedures usually measure certain items by volume, although in the Metric or Imperial systems they are measured by weight. Here are some approximate equivalents for basic items appearing in this book.*

	U.S. Customary	Metric	Imperial
Butter	1 cup	250 g	8 ounces
	½ cup	125 g	4 ounces
	¼ cup	62 g	2 ounces
	1 tablespoon	15 g	½ ounce
Chocolate chips	½ cup	85 g	3 ounces
Coconut (shredded)	½ cup	60 g	2 ounces
Cornstarch	1 teaspoon	10 g	⅓ ounce
Cream of Tartar	1 teaspoon	3–4 g	⅛ ounce
Flour (sifted all-purpose)	1 cup	128 g	4¼ ounces
	½ cup	60 g	2⅛ ounces
	¼ cup	32 g	1 ounce
Fruit (chopped)	1 cup	225 g	8 ounces
Nut Meats (chopped)	1 cup	115 g	4 ounces
Raisins (or sultans)	¾ cup	125 g	4 ounces
Sugar:			
Granulated (Caster)	1 cup	240 g	8 ounces
	½ cup	120 g	4 ounces
	¼ cup	60 g	2 ounces
	1 tablespoon	15 g	½ ounce
Confectioners' (Icing)	1 cup	140 g	5 ounces
	½ cup	70 g	3 ounces
	¼ cup	35 g	1+ ounce
	1 tablespoon	10 g	¼ ounce
Brown	1 cup	160 g	5⅓ ounces
	½ cup	80 g	2⅔ ounces
	¼ cup	40 g	1⅓ ounces
	1 tablespoon	10 g	⅓ ounce

*So as to avoid awkward measurements, some conversions are not exact.

BAR COOKIES

I f you like your cookies easy . . . and quick . . . and delicious . . . then nothing could be simpler than bar cookies. They're also the most versatile of the genre—they can be thick and chewy, thin and crisp or soft and cakelike. Or they might be double-decker cookies, like *Kahlúa Dream Bars*, with a crisp base topped by a chewy layer. Cut into small portions, they're *cookies*; cut into 3-inch squares and topped with ice cream, they become a full-fledged dessert. Whatever the guise, bar cookies are a boon for busy cooks who want delicious results with little effort.

The ingredients for a bar cookie are mixed, spread in a pan and baked . . . that's as hard as it gets! Be sure to use the pan size called for in the recipe. A smaller pan, and your cookies will be too thick and gummy in the middle; a larger pan will produce thin, dry results. Because glass absorbs and retains more heat, always reduce the oven by 25°F when using a glass pan. Some bar cookies may still look soft in the center at the end of the baking time but will firm as they cool. Each of the following recipes gives a guideline for testing doneness; in general, a toothpick inserted in the center should come out clean.

Bar cookies are cooled and usually stored right in the pan. Most are cut *after* they've cooled. The exception to that rule is crisp-style bars, which are cut when warm—before they crisp—to prevent unsightly crumbling. However you cut them . . . however you serve them . . . you're bound to fall in love with this easy answer to almost-instant cookie success!

Almond Butter Fingers

(Mördegspinnar, *from Sweden*)

These buttery, crumbly, nut-coated cookies are the perfect accompaniment for coffee. The original recipe requires forming the dough by hand into long "fingers." This version is much quicker because the cookies are baked in a jelly-roll pan and then simply cut into strips. Almond butter fingers are delicate and should be handled with care.

1 Preheat oven to 275°F. Lightly grease a 10- x 15-inch jelly-roll pan. In a large mixing bowl, beat butter, sugar and salt together until light and fluffy. Beat in egg yolk and almond and vanilla extracts. Stir in cardamom, then flour, ½ cup at a time, blending well after each addition.

2 Use a rubber spatula to spread dough evenly over bottom of prepared pan, or dampen fingers with water and pat dough into place. In a small bowl, lightly whisk egg white until frothy. Pour over dough; spread evenly with the back of a large spoon. Sprinkle nuts over dough and press lightly into surface with the back of a spoon.

3 Bake 50 to 60 minutes, or until golden brown. Immediately use a sharp knife to cut warm cookies into 40 (1- x 3¾-inch) fingers, cutting 10 strips one way and 4 strips the other way. Cool 15 minutes in pan on rack. Carefully remove from pan with a metal spatula; cookies are very fragile. Cool completely on racks. Store in an airtight container at room temperature 1 week; freeze for longer storage.

1 cup butter, softened

1 cup powdered sugar

¼ teaspoon salt

1 egg, separated

¾ teaspoon almond extract

¾ teaspoon vanilla extract

¾ teaspoon ground cardamom

2 cups all-purpose flour

1 cup finely chopped almonds

Makes about 3 dozen cookies

Opposite: Lamington Bars (page 39).
Page following: Linzer Squares (page 42).

Almond Toffee Crisps

(from the United States)

These cookies remind me of chocolate-topped almond toffee candy . . . scrumptious! The topping is made the easy way: The chocolate chips are simply sprinkled over the hot cookie base, and a minute later they are soft enough to spread easily.

1 Preheat oven to 350°F. Grease a 10- x 15-inch jelly- roll pan. In a large mixing bowl, beat butter, brown sugar, vanilla and salt until light and fluffy. In a medium bowl, combine flour and baking soda. Stir into butter mixture ½ cup at a time, blending well after each addition. Spread evenly in prepared pan.

2 Bake 23 to 28 minutes, or until golden brown. Remove from oven; immediately sprinkle chocolate chips over surface of hot cookie base. Cover with a baking sheet, making sure it doesn't touch chocolate. Let stand 1 minute, or until chocolate melts (though melted, the chocolate chips will hold their shape). Use a rubber spatula to spread melted chocolate evenly over cookie base. Immediately sprinkle with almonds and press in lightly with the back of a spoon. Refrigerate 10 minutes, or until chocolate is set. Cut into 50 (1-x 3-inch) strips, cutting 5 strips one way and 10 strips the other way. Cool completely in pan on rack. Store in an airtight container at room temperature 1 week; freeze for longer storage.

Variation
White Chocolate-Almond Toffee Crisps: Substitute 6 ounces white chocolate chips or finely chopped white chocolate for semisweet chocolate chips.

1 cup butter, softened
1 cup packed brown sugar
2 teaspoons vanilla extract
½ teaspoon salt
2 cups all-purpose flour
½ teaspoon baking soda
1 package (6 ounces) semisweet chocolate chips
¾ cup chopped slivered almonds

Makes about 4 dozen cookies

Opposite: Basel Honey Bars (page 54).
Page preceding: Hawaiian Macadamia-
*   Coconut Squares (page 41).*

Butterscotch-Chocolate Chip Chews

(from the United States)

Gooey-chewy-good . . . that's the best way to describe these wonderful cookie bars that will satisfy the most demanding sweet tooth. Both dark brown sugar and dark corn syrup contribute to the butterscotch flavor of the cookie, and a shiny butterscotch glaze gilds the lily. If you want an even more "butter-scotchy" cookie, substitute butterscotch-flavored morsels for the chocolate chips.

1 Preheat oven to 350°F. Grease a 9- x 13-inch baking pan. To prepare Butterscotch Bars: In a medium bowl, combine flour, salt and baking soda; set aside. In a large mixing bowl, beat butter and brown sugar together until light and fluffy. Beat in corn syrup, egg and vanilla. Stir in flour mixture ½ cup at a time, blending well after each addition. Stir in chocolate chips and nuts. Spread evenly in prepared pan.

2 Bake 35 to 45 minutes, or until cookie begins to pull away from sides of pan and a toothpick inserted in the center comes out clean. Cool in pan on rack.

3 To prepare Butterscotch Glaze: Combine all ingredients except vanilla in a heavy medium saucepan. Bring to boil over medium heat, stirring occasionally. Continue to cook 4 minutes, then remove from heat. Cool until barely warm; stir in vanilla. Pour glaze over cooled cookie base. Sprinkle with ½ cup chocolate chips or nuts. Refrigerate 30 minutes before cutting.

4 Cut into 24 (about 2-inch) squares, cutting 4 strips one way and 6 strips the other way.

Butterscotch Bars

2¼ cups all-purpose flour

½ teaspoon salt

½ teaspoon baking soda

¾ cup + 1 tablespoon butter, softened

1¼ cups packed dark brown sugar

½ cup dark corn syrup

1 egg

1 tablespoon vanilla extract

¾ cup semisweet chocolate chips

1½ cups toasted chopped pecans

Butterscotch Glaze

⅓ cup dark corn syrup

½ cup granulated sugar

3 tablespoons whipping cream

2 tablespoons butter

pinch of salt

½ cup miniature semisweet chocolate chips or toasted chopped pecans

2 teaspoons vanilla extract

Makes 2 dozen cookies

Caramel-Pecan Bars

(from the United States)

Patterned after those fabulous candies called "Turtles," these easy bars have a crisp base topped with pecans, a gooey caramel filling and creamy chocolate topping.

1 Preheat oven to 350°F. Grease a 10- x 15-inch jelly- roll pan. To prepare cookie base: In a large mixing bowl, beat butter, brown sugar, vanilla and salt until light and fluffy. Stir in flour ½ cup at a time, blending well after each addition. Spread evenly in prepared pan. Cover solidly with rows of pecan halves.

2 Bake 18 to 22 minutes, or until golden brown. Cool in pan on rack.

3 To prepare filling: In a heavy medium saucepan, combine all ingredients except vanilla. Cook over medium-high heat, stirring occasionally, until mixture reaches 230°F on a candy thermometer, or until mixture forms a 2-inch thread when dropped from a spoon. Immediately remove from heat; stir in vanilla. Pour hot caramel over cookie base and spread evenly. Set aside until cool.

4 To prepare topping: In a medium saucepan, combine chocolate, butter and half & half. Cook over low heat, stirring constantly, until mixture is smooth. Remove from heat and stir in vanilla. Pour over cooled caramel. Let chocolate set before cutting into 60 (about 1½-inch) squares, cutting 6 strips one way and 10 strips the other way. Store in an airtight container at room temperature 1 week; freeze for longer storage.

Cookie Base

⅔ cup butter, softened

1 cup packed brown sugar

1 teaspoon vanilla extract

¼ teaspoon salt

2 cups flour

about 2½ cups pecan halves

Caramel Filling

1⅓ cups packed brown sugar

¾ cup whipping cream

¾ cup light corn syrup

⅓ cup butter

⅛ teaspoon salt

2 teaspoons vanilla extract

Chocolate Topping

10 ounces semisweet chocolate, coarsely chopped

¼ cup butter

3 tablespoons half & half or milk

½ teaspoon vanilla extract

Makes 5 dozen cookies

Canadian Apple-Oat Bars

British Columbia is known for its luscious fruit—apricots, raspberries, peaches, strawberries, pears and especially apples. This cakelike bar cookie has a crisp streusel topping and deliciously showcases Eve's favorite fruit. Be sure to choose tart apples—overly sweet fruit loses a great deal of flavor in the baking. Use regular or quick-cooking rolled oats—not "instant" oatmeal, which turns mushy when exposed to moisture.

1 Preheat oven to 375°F. Grease a 9- x 13-inch baking pan. To prepare streusel: In a medium bowl, combine brown sugar, flour, cinnamon and nutmeg. Using a pastry blender or two knives, cut in butter until mixture resembles coarse crumbs; refrigerate.

2 To prepare cookie base: In a medium bowl, combine oats, flour, baking powder, baking soda, cinnamon, nutmeg, allspice, cloves and salt; set aside. In a large mixing bowl, beat butter and brown sugar together until light and fluffy. Beat in egg. Stir in flour mixture ½ cup at a time, blending well after each addition. Stir in apple and nuts. Spread evenly in prepared pan. Sprinkle top evenly with streusel mixture.

3 Bake 35 to 40 minutes, or until a toothpick inserted in the center comes out clean and cookie begins to pull away from sides of pan. Cool in pan on rack. If desired, dust lightly with powdered sugar. Cut into 24 (about 1½- x 2-inch) rectangles, cutting 4 strips one way and 8 strips the other way. Store in an airtight container at room temperature 1 week; freeze for longer storage.

Streusel Topping
¾ cup packed brown sugar
¼ cup all-purpose flour
¼ teaspoon ground cinnamon
¼ teaspoon ground nutmeg
¼ cup cold butter

Cookie Base
1½ cups rolled oats
1 cup all-purpose flour
½ teaspoon baking powder
½ teaspoon baking soda
½ teaspoon ground cinnamon
½ teaspoon ground nutmeg
½ teaspoon ground allspice
¼ teaspoon ground cloves
¼ teaspoon salt
½ cup butter
1 cup packed brown sugar
1 egg
1½ cups chopped peeled tart apple
1 cup chopped walnuts
powdered sugar, optional

Makes 2 dozen cookies

Cranberry Chews

(from the United States)

Cranberries are grown in huge, sandy bogs on low, trailing vines and—depending on the variety—harvested between Labor Day and Halloween. Though there's no hard evidence, it's a reasonable assumption that the Indians brought baskets of these tart berries to the first Thanksgiving celebration in 1621. This recipe uses canned whole-berry cranberry sauce so you can enjoy these cookie bars year-round.

1 Preheat oven to 350°F. Grease a 10- x 15-inch jelly-roll pan. In a large bowl, combine 2 cups flour, brown sugar, cinnamon, nutmeg, cloves and salt. Use a pastry blender or 2 knives to cut in butter until mixture resembles coarse crumbs, or blend in a food processor using pulses. Stir in oats. Reserve 1½ cups mixture. Firmly press remainder over bottom of prepared pan. Bake 15 minutes. Cool 10 minutes before filling.

2 In a medium bowl, stir together cranberry sauce, marmalade and vanilla. Sift remaining ⅓ cup flour over cranberry mixture 1 tablespoon at a time, blending well after each addition. Spread evenly over baked and cooled crust. Add nuts to reserved oat mixture; sprinkle over top of cranberry filling.

3 Bake about 30 minutes, or until lighty browned. Cool in pan on rack. Cut into 64 (about 1½- x 2-inch) bars, cutting 8 strips both ways. Store in an airtight container at room temperature 1 week; freeze for longer storage.

2⅓ cups all-purpose flour
1 cup packed brown sugar
1 teaspoon ground cinnamon
½ teaspoon ground nutmeg
¼ teaspoon ground cloves
½ teaspoon salt
1 cup cold butter, cut into 16 pieces
1½ cups rolled oats
1 can (16 ounces) whole-berry cranberry sauce
½ cup thick orange marmalade
1 teaspoon vanilla extract
1 cup chopped walnuts

Makes about 5 dozen cookies

Edinburgh Squares

(from Scotland)

Most British cookies (called biscuits) are crisp and crunchy, but an exception to that rule are the chewy, bar-type Edinburgh Squares. Full of fruit, coconut and nuts, these cookie bars are cut small owing to their richness. Finely chopped dried apricots make a nice substitute for either the currants or the cherries. See page 17 for a note about golden syrup.

1 Preheat oven to 375°F. Lightly grease a 10- x 15-inch jelly-roll pan. To prepare cookie base, combine oats, flour, sugar, cinnamon, ginger and salt in a large bowl. Use a pastry blender or two knives to cut in butter until mixture resembles coarse crumbs. Stir in eggs. Turn dough into prepared pan and use a rubber spatula to spread evenly over bottom.

2 Bake cookie base 15 minutes. Remove from oven; cool on rack 10 minutes.

3 To prepare filling, combine currants, cherries, coconut, nuts and ginger in a large bowl; set aside. In a medium bowl, stir together butter, golden syrup and eggs. Add to fruit-nut mixture and stir to combine. Spread evenly over baked crust.

4 Bake 22 to 27 minutes, or until golden brown. Cool on rack.

5 To prepare glaze, combine sugar and golden syrup in a medium bowl. Stir in enough orange juice or milk to make a smooth, creamy glaze of medium consistency. Drizzle glaze over cooled cookies. Let glaze set before cutting into 70 (about 1½-inch) squares, cutting 7 strips one way and 10 strips the other way. Store in an airtight container at room temperature 1 week; freeze for longer storage.

Cookie Base

1½ cups rolled oats

1 cup all-purpose flour

¼ cup granulated sugar

½ teaspoon ground cinnamon

½ teaspoon ground ginger

¼ teaspoon salt

1 cup cold butter, cut into 16 pieces

2 eggs, lightly beaten

Filling

1 cup dried currants

1 cup candied cherries, rinsed in hot water, thoroughly drained and finely chopped

1 cup shredded or flaked coconut

2 cups chopped walnuts

2 tablespoons finely chopped crystallized ginger

½ cup butter, melted and cooled

½ cup Lyle's golden syrup

2 eggs

Golden Glaze

1 cup powdered sugar

1 tablespoon Lyle's golden syrup

1 to 2 tablespoons orange juice or milk

Makes about 6 dozen cookies

Fruited Mazurek Bars

(from Poland)

This fruited version of almond mazurek, *page 188, has a rich apricot-raisin filling with the crunch of toasted walnuts. Though it's not traditional, I drizzle the finished cookies with semisweet chocolate—not only for visual appeal, but because I find chocolate and apricots a particularly luscious combination. For a bolder chocolate statement, try the variation, below.*

1 In a medium saucepan, combine apricots, raisins and orange juice. Bring to a boil. Remove from heat, cover and let stand 1 hour.

2 Meanwhile, preheat oven to 350°F. Grease and flour a 10- x 15-inch jelly-roll pan. Prepare the dough for Polish Almond Strips through step 1. Use your fingers or the back of a wooden spoon to press dough in an even layer over bottom of pan, flouring fingers or spoon lightly if necessary to prevent sticking. Bake 25 minutes, or until golden brown. Remove from oven; let stand 10 minutes before spreading with topping.

3 Stir sugar, nuts and eggs into cooled fruit mixture in pan. Spread evenly over partially baked crust. Bake 25 to 30 minutes, or until edges begin to brown. Cool on rack in pan. Drizzle cookies with melted chocolate. Let chocolate set before cutting into 36 (about 2- x 2-inch) squares, cutting 5 strips one way and 7 strips the other way. Store in an airtight container at room temperature 1 week; freeze for longer storage.

Variation
Chocolate Chip Mazurek Bars: Add 1 (6-ounce) package semisweet chocolate chips to filling mixture before spreading over partially baked crust.

1¾ cups chopped dried apricots
1½ cups dark raisins
1 cup orange juice
1 recipe Crunchy Almond Strips, page 188, with changes noted below
½ cup granulated sugar
1½ cups chopped toasted walnuts
2 eggs, lightly beaten
3 ounces semisweet chocolate, melted and warm

Makes 3 dozen cookies

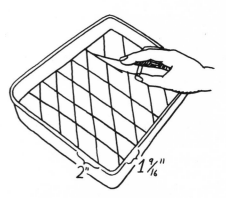

2" 1⁹⁄₁₆"

How to cut 2″ diamonds.

Honeyed Fruit Strips

(Pastine al Miele, *from Italy)*

These semisoft cookies are lightly sweetened with honey. Bits of maraschino cherry add color and toasted almonds lend a delightful crunch. Honeyed Fruit Strips are best when eaten within two to three days. They're wonderful served slightly warm.

1 Preheat oven to 325°F. Grease 1 large baking sheet. In a large bowl, combine flour, baking powder and salt. Use a pastry blender or two knives to cut in butter until mixture resembles coarse crumbs, or process in a food processor using pulses. Add nuts and cherries; toss to combine.

2 In a medium bowl, lightly beat eggs. Add honey and beat to combine. Stir into flour mixture. Knead in bowl 1 minute, or until dough holds together without crumbling.

3 Place dough in center of prepared baking sheet. With buttered fingers, pat out into a 10- x 9-inch rectangle. Brush surface with egg glaze; sprinkle with sugar.

4 Bake 13 to 17 minutes, or just until top springs back when lightly pressed with a fingertip. Let cookie rectangle stand on baking sheet 10 minutes. Use a long, sharp knife to cut into 30 (3- x 1-inch) strips, cutting 3 strips one way and 10 strips the other way. Serve warm or cool on racks. Store in an airtight container at room temperature 2 to 3 days; freeze for longer storage.

2¾ cups all-purpose flour
1½ teaspoons baking powder
½ teaspoon salt
⅓ cup cold butter, cut into 6 pieces
½ cup chopped toasted almonds
½ cup finely chopped maraschino cherries, blotted well on paper towels
2 eggs
⅓ cup honey
1 egg white beaten with 2 teaspoons water for glaze
2-3 tablespoons granulated sugar

Makes 2½ dozen cookies

Kahlúa Dream Bars

(from the United States)

No, it's not a misprint . . . there's ½ cup of Kahlúa in these deliciously heady cookie bars! Let's just say that they're best consumed after the kiddies are tucked in bed. A brown sugar-pecan crust is the base for a chewy, coffee-flavored coconut topping. If you're not a coconut fancier, pecans can be substituted. Serve these cookies warm with vanilla ice cream for a "dreamy" dessert!

1 Preheat oven to 350°F. Grease a 9- x 13-inch baking pan. To prepare cookie base: In a large mixing bowl, beat butter, brown sugar and salt until light and fluffy. Add flour ½ cup at a time, blending well after each addition. Stir in pecans. Spread evenly over bottom of prepared pan. Bake 12 minutes; remove to a rack.

2 To prepare topping: In a small mixing bowl, beat eggs, coffee powder and salt until light. Beating constantly at medium-high speed, add sugars ¼ cup at a time, beating well after each addition. Increase speed to high; continue beating until mixture is thick and pale and ribbons form in bowl when beaters are lifted, 5 to 10 minutes. With mixer running at medium speed, gradually add ½ cup Kahlúa, then flour and baking powder; beat only until combined. Fold in coconut. Pour evenly over partially baked crust.

3 Bake 20 minutes. Remove from oven. If desired, drizzle with remaining 2 tablespoons Kahlúa. Return to oven; bake an additional 5 minutes or until top is set and evenly browned. Cool in pan on rack. Dust cooled cookies with powdered sugar. Cut into 48 (about 1½-inch) squares, cutting 6 strips one way and 8 strips the other way. Store in an airtight container at room temperature 1 week; freeze for longer storage.

Cookie Base

¾ cup butter, softened

¾ cup packed brown sugar

⅛ teaspoon salt

1½ cups all-purpose flour

1 cup chopped toasted pecans

Coconut-Kahlúa Topping

2 eggs

2 teaspoons instant coffee powder

¼ teaspoon salt

½ cup granulated sugar

½ cup packed brown sugar

½ cup Kahlúa or other coffee liqueur

⅓ cup all-purpose flour

1 teaspoon baking powder

1 cup flaked coconut

2 tablespoons additional Kahlúa (optional)

powdered sugar

Makes 4 dozen cookies

Kentucky Bourbon Bars

(from the United States)

"For adults only" is how this wickedly heady cookie bar should be labeled. A goodly splash of bourbon is baked right into the cookie, and the bourbon-spiked frosting adds more old-fashioned "Kentucky" flavor. A delicious triumvirate of pecans, raisins and chocolate chips adds its own magic, and the result is irresistibly naughty . . . but nice!

1 Preheat oven to 350°F. Grease a 9- x 13-inch baking pan. To prepare Bourbon Bars: In a medium bowl, combine flour, baking powder and salt; set aside. In a large mixing bowl, beat butter, brown sugar and vanilla until light and fluffy. Add eggs one at a time, beating well after each addition. Stir in flour mixture and bourbon alternately in 3 additions, blending well after each. Stir in nuts, raisins and chocolate chips. Spread evenly in prepared pan.

2 Bake 20 to 25 minutes, or until a toothpick inserted in the center comes out clean. Cool in pan on rack.

3 To prepare Tipsy Frosting: In a small mixing bowl, beat sugar, butter, vanilla and 3 tablespoons bourbon until smooth. Add enough additional bourbon to make a smooth, creamy frosting of medium consistency. Spread over cooled cookies in pan. Let frosting set before cutting into 24 (about 2-inch) squares, cutting 4 strips one way and 6 strips the other way. If desired, top each square with a pecan half. Store, covered, at room temperature 5 days; freeze for longer storage.

Bourbon Bars

1½ cups all-purpose flour

¾ teaspoon baking powder

¼ teaspoon salt

⅔ cup butter, softened

¾ cup packed brown sugar

1½ teaspoons vanilla extract

2 eggs

⅓ cup bourbon

1 cup chopped toasted pecans

½ cup raisins

½ cup semisweet chocolate chips

Tipsy Frosting

3½ cups powdered sugar

6 tablespoons butter, softened

1 teaspoon vanilla extract

3 to 5 tablespoons bourbon or half milk and half bourbon

24 pecan halves (optional)

Makes 2 dozen cookies

Lamington Bars

(from Australia)

Australia's famous Lamingtons are squares of sponge cake that are first dipped in a chocolate glaze and then in coconut. This cookie version of that wonderful dessert has the same chocolate-coconut coating, but the inside is denser and loaded with lots of toasted almonds.

1 Preheat oven to 375°F. Grease a 10- x 15-inch jelly- roll pan. Place a 22-inch length of waxed paper lengthwise in pan. Smooth paper so it conforms to pan, allowing excess to hang over ends of pan. Butter the waxed paper. In a medium bowl, combine flour, baking powder and salt; set aside. In a large mixing bowl, beat butter, sugar and vanilla until light and fluffy. Add eggs one at a time, beating well after each addition. Stir in flour mixture ½ cup at a time, blending well after each addition. Stir in nuts. Spread evenly in prepared pan.

2 Bake 10 to 15 minutes, or just until a toothpick inserted in the center comes out clean. Holding ends of waxed paper, lift cookie base out of pan and place on rack. Cool.

3 To prepare glaze: In a large bowl, whisk together powdered sugar and cocoa until no lumps remain. Add vanilla and 4 tablespoons milk. Add enough of the remaining milk to make a smooth, creamy glaze of medium consistency.

4 Line a large baking sheet with waxed paper. Place coconut on a large plate. Cut cookie base into 48 (1¼- x 2½-inch) strips. Use a fork to spear cookie rectangles; dip into chocolate glaze, allowing excess to drip back into bowl. Place chocolate-dipped cookie on plate of coconut; use 2 forks to turn cookie so that all sides are coated. Place on prepared baking sheet and refrigerate until glaze is set. Store in an airtight container at room temperature 1 week; freeze for longer storage.

2 cups all-purpose flour
1 teaspoon baking powder
¼ teaspoon salt
¾ cup butter, softened
¾ cup granulated sugar
1 teaspoon vanilla extract
3 eggs
1 cup finely chopped toasted walnuts
about 5 cups flaked coconut (one 14-ounce package)
Chocolate Glaze
6 cups powdered sugar
⅔ cup unsweetened cocoa powder
2 teaspoons vanilla extract
10 to 12 tablespoons milk

Makes 4 dozen cookies

Lemon Cheesecake Bars

(from the United States)

If you've never tried the flavors of chocolate and lemon together, you're in for an exotic taste sensation! Those who prefer a more traditional approach may choose the lemon glaze for these spritely bars with a cheesecake-style filling. These cookie bars must be prepared in advance and refrigerated overnight.

1 Preheat oven to 350°F. Grease a 9- x 13-inch baking pan. In a medium bowl, combine flour, powdered sugar and salt. Use a pastry blender or 2 knives to cut in butter until mixture resembles coarse crumbs, or blend in a food processor using pulses. Stir in chopped almonds. Press firmly over bottom of prepared pan. Bake 15 minutes. Cool 10 minutes before topping with cheese mixture.

2 In a large mixing bowl, beat cream cheese and sugar until smooth. Add eggs one at a time, beating well after each addition. Beat in lemon juice and vanilla. Pour over baked crust.

3 Bake 22 to 28 minutes, or until firm. Cool in pan on rack to room temperature. Prepare Chocolate Glaze or Lemon Glaze. *To prepare Lemon Glaze*: In a medium bowl, combine powdered sugar, vanilla and milk. Add enough lemon juice to to make a thick, smooth glaze. Pour glaze of your choice over cheesecake base; smooth surface. Sprinkle with sliced almonds. Cover and refrigerate overnight before cutting.

4 Use a sharp, thin-bladed knife to cut 24 (about 2-inch) squares, cutting 4 strips one way and 6 strips the other way. Wipe the knife with a paper towel between cuts to prevent getting excess cheesecake mixture into the glaze. Store airtight *in refrigerator* 5 days. Do not freeze.

1½ cups all-purpose flour

⅔ cup powdered sugar

¼ teaspoon salt

¾ cup cold butter, cut into 12 pieces

¾ cup chopped toasted almonds

2 packages (8 ounces each) cream cheese, softened

⅔ cup granulated sugar

3 eggs

⅓ cup fresh lemon juice

½ teaspoon vanilla extract

Chocolate Glaze, page 39, or Lemon Glaze, below

⅓ cup sliced toasted almonds

Lemon Glaze

2½ cups powdered sugar

½ teaspoon vanilla extract

1 tablespoon milk

2 to 4 tablespoons fresh lemon juice

Makes 2 dozen cookies

Hawaiian Macadamia-Coconut Squares

My sister Tia first introduced me to macadamia nuts years ago, after she toured Hawaii as Miss Colorado. Instant coffee powder adds intrigue to these rich, chewy bars, which are freighted with macadamia nuts. Believe it or not, the macadamia tree was first used as an ornamental shrub! It took its name from John MacAdam, a Scottish-born chemist who cultivated the plant in Australia. The 1890s saw the macadamia tree journey from Tasmania to Hawaii, where it's now the third-largest crop.

1 Preheat oven to 325°F. Grease a 9- x 13-inch baking pan; set aside. In a large mixing bowl, beat butter, 1 cup brown sugar, instant coffee powder, ¼ teaspoon cinnamon and ¼ teaspoon salt until light and fluffy. Stir in flour ½ cup at a time, blending well after each addition. Spread evenly in prepared pan. Bake 20 minutes. Cool in pan on rack 15 minutes.

2 In a large bowl, beat eggs and vanilla with remaining 1 cup brown sugar, ¼ teaspoon cinnamon and ¼ teaspoon salt. Stir in coconut and macadamias. Spread evenly over cooled baked layer. Bake 40 to 50 minutes, or until golden brown and firm to the touch.

3 Use a knife to loosen cookies around edges while warm. Cool completely in pan on rack. Cut into 48 (about 1½-inch) squares, cutting 6 strips one way and 8 strips the other way. Store in an airtight container at room temperature 1 week; freeze for longer storage.

1 cup butter, softened
2 cups packed brown sugar
1 tablespoon instant coffee powder
½ teaspoon ground cinnamon
½ teaspoon salt
2 cups all-purpose flour
3 eggs
2 teaspoons vanilla extract
2 cups shredded or flaked coconut
2 cups chopped toasted macadamia nuts

Makes 4 dozen cookies

Linzer Squares

(Linzer Törtchen, from Austria)

This is a cookie version of the classic Viennese Linzertorte. Almonds may be substituted for the hazelnuts with equally delicious results. My version of Linzer Squares has a nontraditional (but scrumptious) chocolate layer between the cookie base and the raspberry jam. A sugar-glazed lattice crust crowns these showstoppers to create a cookie that's as stunningly beautiful as it is delicious!

1 Lightly grease an 8- x 8-inch square baking pan. In a medium bowl, combine flour, ground hazelnuts, cinnamon, cloves and salt; set aside. In a large mixing bowl, beat butter and sugar together until light and fluffy. Beat in egg yolk, vanilla and lemon zest. Stir in flour mixture ½ cup at a time, blending well after each addition.

2 Form 1 cup of the dough into a flat square. Place between 2 large sheets of waxed paper and roll out to an 8-inch square. If necessary, trim edges. Place dough square in waxed paper on a baking sheet; freeze 10 to 15 minutes. If desired, add chopped hazelnuts to remaining dough. Press remaining dough evenly over bottom of prepared pan. Spoon melted chocolate over dough and spread evenly with the back of a spoon. Refrigerate 5 minutes, or until chocolate is set. Spread jam over chocolate to within ¼ inch of edges.

3 Preheat oven to 375°. Remove dough square from freezer. Peel off top piece of waxed paper. Cut dough into 16 (8- x ½-inch) strips. *Lightly* brush strips with egg glaze; sprinkle with decorating sugar. Starting at edge of pan, lay 8 dough strips, ½ inch apart, vertically over jam. Place remaining 8 strips crosswise over first layer, creating a lattice effect.

2 cups all-purpose flour
¾ cup finely ground hazelnuts
¾ teaspoon ground cinnamon
⅛ teaspoon ground cloves
¼ teaspoon salt
⅔ cup butter, softened
⅔ cup granulated sugar
1 egg yolk
1 teaspoon vanilla extract
finely grated zest of 1 large lemon
½ cup chopped hazelnuts (optional)
2 ounces semisweet chocolate, melted and cooled to room temperature
⅔ cup seedless red raspberry jam, stirred until smooth
1 egg white beaten with 2 teaspoons water for glaze
about 2 tablespoons coarse decorating sugar

Makes 16 cookies

4 Bake about 30 minutes, or until golden brown. Cool in pan on rack. Cut into 16 (2-inch) squares, cutting 4 strips each way. Use a paper towel to wipe the knife after each cut to prevent jam or chocolate from smearing on pastry lattice. Store in an airtight container at room temperature 1 week; freeze for longer storage.

Orange Congo Squares

(from the United States)

I have no idea where these big, chewy bars got their exotic name but I do know the recipe's been around for ages. My version is different in that it uses twice the amount of chocolate chips. And, because it goes so well with chocolate, I've added fresh orange zest and orange juice concentrate. It's important not to overbake these bars—they'll lose their deliciously moist chewiness.

1 Preheat oven to 350°F. Grease a 10- x 15-inch jelly-roll pan. In a medium bowl, combine flour, baking powder, baking soda and salt; set aside. In a large bowl, combine eggs, oil, orange juice concentrate and sugar and beat until well combined. Stir in orange zest, then flour mixture, ½ cup at a time, blending well after each addition. Add 1 cup nuts and all but 1/3 cup chocolate chips; stir to combine. Turn into in prepared pan; smooth surface. Sprinkle with remaining ⅓ cup nuts and ⅓ cup chocolate chips.

2 Bake 25 to 30 minutes, or until deep golden brown. Do not overbake; cooled cookies should be soft and chewy. Cool in pan on rack. Cut into 24 (2½-inch) squares, cutting 4 strips one way and 6 strips the other way. Store in an airtight container at room temperature 1 week; freeze for longer storage.

Variation
Coconut-Orange Congo Squares: Reduce brown sugar to 1½ cups packed; add 1 cup shredded or flaked coconut with chocolate chips and nuts.

2¾ cups all-purpose flour

2 teaspoons baking powder

½ teaspoon baking soda

¼ teaspoon salt

3 eggs

½ cup vegetable oil

¼ cup frozen orange juice concentrate, thawed

1 box (1 pound) brown sugar (about 2¼ cups packed)

grated zest of 1 medium orange

1⅓ cups chopped toasted pecans or walnuts, divided

1 package (12 ounces) semisweet chocolate chips

Makes about 2 dozen cookies

Opposite: Chocolate-Dipped Sablés (page 51).
Page following: Coconut Shortbread (page 56).

Orange Marmalade-Cream Cheese Bars

(from the United States)

As with all cooking and baking, quality ingredients produce a superior result. In this instance, it's particularly important to use a good orange marmalade; inexpensive brands deliver little flavor, too little fruit and too much sweetness. If you can't find a full-flavored marmalade, add grated orange.

1 Preheat oven to 350°F. Grease a 9- x 13-inch baking pan. In a small mixing bowl, beat butter, sugar and salt until light and fluffy. Stir in flour ½ cup at a time, blending well after each addition. Stir in 1 cup of the nuts (mixture will be crumbly). Transfer 1 cup of this mixture to a small bowl. Add remaining ⅓ cup chopped nuts; set aside for topping. Firmly press remaining mixture over bottom of prepared pan in an even layer. Bake 15 minutes.

2 While cookie base is cooling, beat cream cheese in a large mixing bowl until perfectly smooth. Add eggs one at a time, beating well after each addition. Stir in vanilla and ¾ cup marmalade. Spread cooled cookie base with remaining ¾ cup marmalade. Pour cream cheese mixture over top; smooth surface. Sprinkle with reserved nut mixture.

3 Bake 20 to 25 minutes, or until center looks set. Cool to room temperature in pan on rack. Cover and refrigerate 3 hours. Cut into 24 (about 2-inch) squares, cutting 4 strips one way and 6 strips the other way.

¾ cup butter, softened
¾ cup granulated sugar
¼ teaspoon salt
2 cups all-purpose flour
1⅓ cups chopped toasted pecans
12 ounces cream cheese, softened
2 eggs
1 teaspoon vanilla extract
1½ cups orange marmalade

Makes about 2 dozen cookies

Opposite: Hazelnut Spirals (page 64).
Page preceding: Ginger-Rum Biscuits (page 62).

Spicy Date Cakes

(Tamriah, *from Saudi Arabia*)

The fruit of the date palm is particularly popular in the Middle East. Its name comes from the Greek daktulos *(finger), after the shape of the fruit. These tender, cakelike bar cookies are easy to make if you use packaged chopped dates—a real time-saver. Because they're rich, Spicy Date Cakes are cut into small squares. They're absolutely delectable with vanilla ice cream!*

1 Preheat oven to 375°F. Grease and flour a 10- x 15-inch jelly-roll pan. In a large mixing bowl, beat eggs, salt and vanilla until light. Beating constantly at medium speed, add sugar ¼ cup at a time, beating well after each addition. Increase speed to high and continue beating until mixture is thick and pale and ribbons form in bowl when beaters are lifted, 5 to 10 minutes.

2 Meanwhile, combine dates, almonds, flour and spices in a medium bowl. Fold into beaten eggs ½ cup at a time. Spread mixture evenly in prepared pan. Sprinkle with sliced almonds.

3 Bake 14 to 17 minutes, or until dark golden brown. Cool in pan on rack. Cut into 60 (about 1½-inch) squares, cutting 6 strips one way and 10 strips the other way. Store in an airtight container at room temperature 1 week; freeze for longer storage.

4 eggs
¼ teaspoon salt
½ teaspoon vanilla extract
1¼ cups powdered sugar
1½ cups chopped dates
1 cup ground toasted almonds
½ cup all-purpose flour
¼ teaspoon each ground cinnamon, nutmeg and cloves
⅓ cup butter, melted and cooled
½ cup sliced almonds

Makes 5 dozen cookies

ROLLED COOKIES

For me, rolled cookies always awaken sweet, nostalgic memories of my childhood. These were the cookies that kept the Tyler girls (Mom, Tia and me) occupied and out of the cold on many a winter afternoon—rolling, cutting, decorating and, best of all, eating! The rolled cookies I grew up with were usually rather thin. In researching cookies from around the world, however, I found they come in many sizes. For instance, one of my favorites—England's *Fat Rascals*—are, as the name implies, a full half-inch thick!

Simply put, rolled cookies are made by using a rolling pin to flatten the dough, which is then cut into interesting shapes. The main caution when rolling out dough is not to overflour the work surface. The dough will absorb excess flour, making the finished cookies less tender. Dough scraps should be gathered and rerolled at one time; these cookies will never be quite as tender owing to the extra handling. Because I use a textured acrylic pastry board, which is virtually nonstick, I rarely have a problem with overflouring. If you're concerned about it, roll the dough out between 2 sheets of waxed paper or plastic wrap.

The next step is cutting the dough into decorative shapes. You can use cookie cutters, or cut unusual shapes with a pinked or plain-edged pastry wheel, or trace around cardboard patterns with a knife. Dip cutters or knife into flour or granulated sugar if they begin to stick to the dough. Cut cookies as close together as possible to prevent excess scraps. And, lastly, have fun making memories with these beautiful, delicious treats!

Jam Rings

(Ischler Törtchen, *from Austria*)

Ground almonds or hazelnuts add intrigue to these rich Austrian sandwich cookies. One version features a generous dusting of powdered sugar surrounding a center of sparkling red jam. Any flavor of jam will do, but the brighter the color, the prettier the cookie. Another version, preferred by all my chocolate-loving friends, crowns each cookie with a rich chocolate glaze.

1 In a large mixing bowl, beat butter, granulated sugar and vanilla together until light and fluffy. Beat in egg yolks. Gradually stir in flour, then nuts (dough will be crumbly). Knead dough in bowl for 30 seconds; form into a ball. Cover and refrigerate 1 hour.

2 Preheat oven to 325°F. Grease 4 large baking sheets. On a floured surface, roll out dough to ³⁄₁₆-inch thickness. Using a 2-inch cutter, cut dough into as many circles as you can. Form leftover scraps into a ball; reroll and cut. Use a ½-inch cookie cutter (or the cap from a small bottle of flavoring extract) to cut out the center of half the dough circles. Form leftover dough into ball; reroll and cut. Arrange circles and rings, 1 inch apart, on prepared baking sheets.

3 Bake 12 to 18 minutes, or until golden brown. Carefully transfer cookies to racks to cool. Stir jam or jelly until smooth. Spread top of each solid cookie circle with a thin layer of jam. *Generously* sift powdered sugar over tops of cookie rings. Place a sugared ring cookie on each jam-covered round, lightly pressing the two cookies together to make a sandwich. Handle cookie rings carefully, as they are very delicate. Spoon a dab of jam into the opening of each cookie. Store in an airtight container at room tem-

2 cups butter, softened
1½ cups granulated sugar
2 teaspoons vanilla extract
4 egg yolks
4 cups all-purpose flour
2½ cups ground almonds or hazelnuts
about 1 cup seedless red raspberry or strawberry jam or jelly
powdered sugar

Makes about 3 dozen cookies

perature 5 days; freeze for longer storage. Place a piece of waxed paper between layers in storage container.

Variation

Chocolate-Glazed Jam Cookies: Cut all cookie dough into solid circles (without center holes). Bake and cool as directed. Spread bottom cookie with jam; top with second cookie. Set cookies on a rack over waxed paper. Spoon about 2 teaspoons Bittersweet Chocolate Glaze (recipe below) over each cookie, spreading with the back of a spoon if necessary. Let glaze set before serving or storing.

Combine all ingredients in top of double boiler set over simmering water. Heat, stirring occasionally, until melted and smooth. Remove from heat; cool 20 minutes at room temperature. Stir before using.

Bittersweet Chocolate Glaze

12 ounces semisweet chocolate
¼ cup butter
¼ cup milk
2 tablespoons light corn syrup

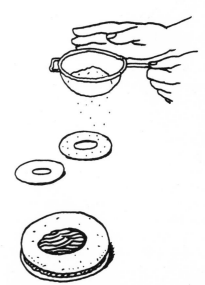

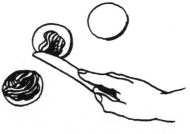

Bakestone Cakes

(from Wales)

I like to bake these lightly sweet, currant-studded cookies the old-fashioned way . . . on a griddle! But I've also given you today's oven method, which produces a crisper cookie. Either version is terrific with tea! Griddle-baked cookies don't keep as long as the oven-baked version. I solve that handicap by freezing half of the cut-out dough—so I can have fresh Bakestone Cakes whenever I want!

1 In a large bowl, combine flour, sugar, baking powder, nutmeg and salt. Use a pastry blender or 2 knives to cut in butter until mixture resembles coarse crumbs, or process in a food processor using pulses. Stir in currants and lemon zest. In a small bowl, lightly beat eggs and milk together; stir into flour mixture. Form dough into a ball, cover and set aside for 10 minutes.

2 On a well-floured surface, roll dough out into a rough circle ⅛ inch thick. Cut out dough using a 3-inch cutter. Gather and reroll dough scraps. If desired, wrap and freeze half the cutouts, placing a square of waxed paper or plastic wrap between cookies. Bring to room temperature before baking.

3 Lightly butter a large, heavy griddle or skillet; preheat over medium-low heat 3 minutes. Arrange dough cutouts, 1 inch apart, on hot griddle. Bake until golden brown, about 1 minute. Turn and bake second side. If necessary, butter griddle between batches. Cool on racks.

Variation

To oven-bake: Preheat oven to 350°F. Grease 2 large baking sheets. Arrange cutouts, 1 inch apart, on prepared baking sheets. Bake 13 to 16 minutes, or until golden brown on the bottoms.

2 cups all-purpose flour
⅔ cup granulated sugar
1 tablespoon baking powder
½ teaspoon ground nutmeg
¼ teaspoon salt
¼ cup cold butter, cut into 4 pieces
¾ cup dried currants
finely grated zest of 1 large lemon or 1 medium orange
2 eggs
¼ cup milk
1 egg white beaten with 2 teaspoons water for glaze (optional)

Makes about 3½ dozen cookies

Chocolate-Dipped Sablés

(Sablés de Caen, from France)

Popular throughout France, this classic cookie is said to hail from Caen, in the province of Normandy. The French word sablé *means "sand," and the cookies are so named because of their fine, crumbly texture. Dipping the sablés in chocolate is* not *traditional, but the dark chocolate flavor pairs magically with the orange zest to create a delicious culinary* ménage à deux.

1 In a medium bowl, combine flour, sugar, sieved egg yolks, salt and orange zest. Use a pastry blender or two knives to cut in butter until mixture resembles coarse crumbs, or process in a food processor using pulses. Form dough into a ball. Wrap and set aside at room temperature 1 hour.

2 Grease 2 large baking sheets. On a lightly floured surface, roll dough out into a rough circle a scant ¼ inch thick. Cut out dough using a floured decorative or plain 2½-inch round cutter. Gather and reroll dough scraps. Arrange rounds, 1 inch apart, on prepared baking sheets. Refrigerate 15 minutes to firm dough.

3 Preheat oven to 375°F. Bake cookies 9 to 12 minutes, or until golden brown around the edges. Cool on racks.

4 Line 2 large baking sheets with waxed paper; set aside. Turn warm melted chocolate into a deep, small bowl. Dip one cookie at a time halfway into chocolate, shaking off excess. Arrange on prepared baking sheets. Refrigerate until chocolate sets, about 10 minutes.

5 Store cookies in an airtight container at cool room temperature 5 days; freeze for longer storage. In hot weather, store in refrigerator.

1¾ cups all-purpose flour

½ cup granulated sugar

4 hard-cooked egg yolks, sieved

¼ teaspoon salt

finely grated zest of 1 small orange

¾ cup cold butter, cut into 12 pieces

8 ounces semisweet chocolate, melted and warm

Makes about 2½ dozen cookies

Belgian Spice Cookies
(Speculaas)

This rich, spicy cookie is a favorite in Belgium as well as Holland and Germany. Traditionally, the dough is pressed into wooden Speculaas molds, which are carved into designs such as animals, windmills and St. Nicholas. Since the cookies "reflect" the image of the mold, they're called Speculaas, or "mirrors." The molds—from small to giant—are available at gourmet shops and specialty bakeware departments. Never fear, though—these cookies are just as delicious when the dough is simply rolled and cut with a cookie cutter or knife.

1 Preheat oven to 350°F. Grease 2 large baking sheets. In a medium bowl, combine flour, baking powder, spices, salt and pepper; set aside. In a large mixing bowl, cream butter and sugar together until light and fluffy. Add lemon zest and eggs, one at a time, beating well after each addition. Add flour mixture, ½ cup at a time, blending well after each addition. Turn dough out onto a well-floured surface and form into a ball. Cover and let stand 5 minutes.

2 *If using* Speculaas *molds*, generously dust molds with flour, making sure flour gets into crevices. Invert molds and tap out excess flour. Press dough into molds; level off with a thin-bladed knife. Unmold by inverting the mold over the prepared cookie sheet and firmly tapping. If necessary, use the tip of a pointed knife to loosen edge of dough.

3 *To roll out cookies*, work with half the dough at a time. On a floured surface, roll one half of dough out into an 18- x 7-inch rectangle ¼ inch thick. Cut into 2- x 3½-inch rectangles, or use floured cookie cutters to cut into desired shapes.

4½ cups all-purpose flour
1½ teaspoons baking powder
1½ teaspoons ground cinnamon
¾ teaspoon ground nutmeg
½ teaspoon ground cloves
½ teaspoon ground cardamom
¼ teaspoon ground ginger
¾ teaspoon salt
½ teaspoon white pepper
1¼ cups butter, softened
2 cups granulated sugar
finely grated zest of 1 medium lemon
2 eggs
1 egg white beaten with 2 teaspoons water for glaze, (optional)

***Makes about 3 dozen
2- x 3½-inch cookies***

4 Arrange cookies, 1½ inches apart, on prepared baking sheets. If desired, brush tops with egg glaze. Bake until golden brown, 6 to 12 minutes, depending on thickness and size. Cool on racks. Store in an airtight container at room temperature 1 week; freeze for longer storage.

Variation
Add ¾ cup finely ground almonds to flour mixture.

Basel Honey Bars

(Basler Leckerli, *from Switzerland*)

Switzerland is known the world over for its delicious Leckerli. *There are many versions, but the two most popular are from Bern (using ground nuts) and this Basel version, which uses honey. The dough can either be imprinted with a design using a* Leckerli *or* Springerle *mold, cut into bars or cut with a cookie cutter. This traditional recipe from Basel requires the cookies to stand overnight. These cookies are better when allowed to mellow for a week, so plan ahead!* Leckerli *are rather hard, and some people like them that way. I prefer them soft, however, and get that result by putting a couple of apple wedges in the storage container with the cookies.*

1 In a medium bowl, combine flour, cinnamon, cloves and salt; set aside.

2 In a medium saucepan, combine honey and sugar. Bring to a boil over medium heat, then immediately remove from heat without allowing to boil further. Stir in candied peel and lemon zest. Let stand 10 minutes to cool. Stir in Kirsch, ground almonds and chopped almonds or hazelnuts. Add flour mixture 1 cup at a time, stirring until well combined after each addition. Form dough into a ball, cover and let stand 20 minutes.

3 Generously grease 2 large baking sheets. *If using Leckerli or Springerle molds*, generously dust molds with flour. Press dough into molds and level off with a thin-bladed knife. Unmold by inverting the mold over the prepared cookie sheet and tapping; if necessary, use the tip of a pointed knife to loosen the edge of the dough. Brush excess flour from surface of cookies.

4 *To roll out cookies*, work with half the dough at a time. On a floured surface, roll out dough to ½-inch thickness. Use a

4¾ cups all-purpose flour
2 teaspoons ground cinnamon
1½ teaspoons ground cloves
¼ teaspoon salt
1 cup honey
1⅓ cups granulated sugar
½ cup candied citrus peel, finely chopped
finely grated zest of 1 large lemon
⅓ cup + 1 tablespoon Kirsch or good-quality cherry brandy
¾ cup ground almonds
1 cup finely chopped almonds or hazelnuts

Glaze

¼ cup Kirsch or good-quality cherry brandy
½ cup powdered sugar
2 tablespoons honey

Makes about 2 dozen 2-inch cookies

54

floured heart-shaped or other decorative cutter to cut out dough, or roll the dough out to a 12- x 6-inch rectangle, ½ inch thick, and cut into 12 (2- x 3-inch) bars. Arrange cookies, ¼ inch apart, on prepared baking sheets. Cover with waxed paper and set aside overnight in a cool, dry place. Do not refrigerate.

5 Preheat oven to 350°F. Prepare glaze by combining all ingredients in a small saucepan. Bring to a boil, then remove from heat and stir until sugar is dissolved. Let cool to room temperature.

6 Bake cookies 10 minutes, or until golden brown on the bottom. Brush glaze over warm cookies. Cool on racks. Store in airtight containers at room temperature for 1 week before serving. If soft cookies are desired, put 1-2 apple wedges in the storage container with them. Store airtight at room temperature up to 3 weeks; freeze for longer storage.

Coconut Shortbread

(from the Fiji Islands)

Sugar cane and coconut are the major crops of the Fiji Islands, so it's only natural that Fijian cooks created this delightful shortbread. Dipping them in chocolate, however, is my own touch. Coconut and chocolate are such compatible partners that I couldn't resist adding a little adornment to this deliciously rich and crumbly cookie. No one's complained so far!

1 In a medium bowl, combine flour, baking powder and salt; set aside. In a small mixing bowl, beat butter, sugar and vanilla together until light and fluffy. Stir in flour mixture ½ cup at a time, blending well after each addition. Stir in coconut. Form dough into a 4- x 7-inch rectangle. Wrap and freeze or refrigerate until firm, 1 to 4 hours.

2 Preheat oven to 300°F. Grease 2 large baking sheets. On a floured surface, roll dough out into an 8- x 14-inch rectangle about ¼ inch thick. Using a floured knife with a long blade, cut dough into 24 (2-inch) squares, cutting 4 strips one way and 7 strips the other way. Arrange squares, 1 inch apart, on prepared baking sheets.

3 Bake 25 to 30 minutes, or until golden. Cool on racks.

4 Line 2 large baking sheets with waxed paper; set aside. Turn melted chocolate mixture into a small deep bowl. Dip half of each cookie diagonally into chocolate, shaking off excess. Arrange on prepared baking sheets. Refrigerate until chocolate sets, about 10 minutes.

5 Store in an airtight container at room temperature 1 week; freeze for longer storage.

1¾ cups all-purpose flour
½ teaspoon baking powder
¼ teaspoon salt
¾ cup butter, softened
⅓ cup granulated sugar
1½ teaspoons vanilla extract
1 cup flaked coconut
6 ounces semisweet chocolate melted with 2 teaspoons vegetable oil

Makes 2 dozen cookies

Corn Pone Cakes

(from Barbados)

In Barbados there's a popular cornmeal cake that is similar to a light corn-bread, except sweeter. Corn Pone Cakes, scented with rum and dotted with raisins and cherries, are the cookie version of that dessert. The cornmeal gives these thick, dense cookies a pleasantly chewy texture.

1 In a medium bowl, stir together cornmeal, rum, eggs and vanilla. Set aside at room temperature 20 minutes.

2 In a medium bowl, combine flour, nutmeg, cinnamon, baking powder and salt; set aside. In a large mixing bowl, beat butter and sugar together until light. Add cornmeal mixture and beat 1 minute at medium speed. Stir in flour mixture, then raisins and cherries.

3 Preheat oven to 350°F. Grease 2 large baking sheets. On a well-floured surface, roll dough out into a rough circle ½ inch thick. (Dough will be sticky, but use as little flour as possible.) Cut out dough using a floured 2-inch cutter. If necessary, brush excess flour from surface of rounds. Gather scraps into a ball; reroll and cut. Arrange, 1 inch apart, on prepared baking sheets.

4 Bake about 15 minutes, or just until golden brown on the bottom; the tops will not color.

5 While cookies are baking, prepare glaze: Combine glaze ingredients in a small saucepan. Cook over medium heat, stirring constantly, *just* until sugar dissolves. Brush hot glaze over hot cookies while still on baking sheets. Transfer cookies to racks to cool. Store in an airtight container at room temperature 1 week; freeze for longer storage.

1 cup yellow cornmeal
¼ cup dark or light rum
2 eggs, lightly beaten
½ teaspoon vanilla extract
2¼ cups all-purpose flour
¼ teaspoon ground nutmeg
¼ teaspoon ground cinnamon
½ teaspoon baking powder
¼ teaspoon salt
½ cup butter, softened
⅔ cup granulated sugar
½ cup golden raisins
¼ cup chopped maraschino cherries, blotted well on paper towels

Rum Glaze

⅔ cup powdered sugar
⅓ cup dark or light rum

Makes about 1½ dozen 2-inch cookies

Cream Cheese Cookies

(Kolacky, *from Czechoslovakia*)

Cream cheese adds tenderness to these soft, rich cookies with a honey-nut filling. Developed in 1872, cream cheese is so named because of its smooth, spreadable texture. It's made from cow's milk and should contain at least 33 percent butterfat to be called cream cheese. Don't substitute "low-fat" cream cheese in this recipe—the added moisture and lower butterfat will create a cookie that is less than tender.

1 In a medium bowl, combine flour, baking powder and salt; set aside. In a large mixing bowl, beat butter, cream cheese, sugar and vanilla until light and fluffy. Stir in flour mixture ½ cup at a time, blending well after each addition. Cover and refrigerate overnight.

2 Preheat oven to 350°F. If using Honey-Nut Filling: In a medium bowl, stir together nuts, cinnamon and enough honey to make a thick paste; set aside.

3 Divide dough in half; return one half to refrigerator. On a floured surface, roll half of dough out into a rough circle ⅜ inch thick. Cut out dough using a floured 2½-inch cutter. Gather and reroll dough scraps. Repeat with second half of dough. Arrange rounds, 1 inch apart, on 2 to 3 large *ungreased* baking sheets. Use your thumb to make a deep 1-inch-wide indentation in the center of each round. Fill indentation with about 1 teaspoon Honey-Nut Filling or raspberry jam; do not overfill indentations, or filling will spread and create an unattractive cookie.

4 Bake 13 to 15 minutes, or until pale golden brown on the bottom. Cool on racks. Store in an airtight container at room temperature 1 week; freeze for longer storage.

2 cups all-purpose flour

1 teaspoon baking powder

¼ teaspoon salt

1 cup butter, softened

8 ounces cream cheese, softened

⅔ cup granulated sugar

1 teaspoon vanilla extract

Honey-Nut Filling (below) or about
⅔ cup seedless red raspberry
jam

Honey-Nut Filling

1 cup ground walnuts

¾ teaspoon ground cinnamon

about ⅓ cup honey

Makes about 2½ dozen cookies

Fat Rascals

(from England)

A favorite teatime biscuit, this old Yorkshire recipe creates a crisp, buttery cookie that's one of my favorites in this book. Filled with currants, Fat Rascals are wonderful with a steaming hot cup of tea. If the currants you have are hard, cover them with boiling water and let stand 10 minutes to rehydrate. Drain well before using.

1 Preheat oven to 400°F. Generously grease 2 large baking sheets. In a medium bowl, combine flour, brown sugar, baking powder, cinnamon and salt. Add butter and rub into flour mixture with your fingers until mixture resembles fine crumbs. Stir in currants and enough milk to make a soft dough. Gather dough and form into a ball.

2 On a well-floured surface with a floured rolling pin, roll dough out into a rough circle ½ inch thick. Cut out dough using a 2-inch cutter. Form scraps into a ball; roll and cut. Brush excess flour from surface of cookies with a pastry brush. Sprinkle lightly with granulated sugar. Arrange, 1½ inches apart, on prepared baking sheets.

3 Bake 16 to 20 minutes, or until golden brown. Cool on racks. Store in an airtight container at room temperature 1 week; freeze for longer storage.

2 cups all-purpose flour
½ cup packed brown sugar
¾ teaspoon baking powder
1 teaspoon ground cinnamon
⅛ teaspoon salt
⅔ cup butter, cut into 6 pieces and softened
⅔ cup dried currants
2–4 tablespoons milk
granulated sugar

Makes about 1½ dozen cookies

Fruited Cornmeal Cookies

(Gialletti, *from Italy*)

Cornmeal adds natural sweetness and gives these beautiful cookies a wonderful, crunchy texture. If you want a cookie with less texture, grind the cornmeal in a food processor or blender until very fine. The dough can be cut into squares or diamonds; see page 35. Gialletti can be dusted with powdered sugar or, for those with a sweeter tooth, dipped into a glaze and sprinkled with nonpareils or pine nuts.

1 In a large bowl, combine flour, cornmeal and baking powder. Add raisins and blend together until pieces are separated; set aside. In a small mixing bowl, beat butter, sugar and salt together until light. Add rum 1 tablespoon at a time, beating well after each addition. Beat in orange zest and vanilla. Add flour mixture and stir to combine. Form dough into a ball, cover and refrigerate 30 minutes.

2 Preheat oven to 350°F. Grease 3 large baking sheets. Divide dough in half; refrigerate one half. On a floured surface, roll one portion of dough out into a 10½- x 6-inch rectangle, ¼ inch thick. Cut into diamonds (see page 35) with 1½-inch sides. Gather scraps; add to second half of dough. Repeat rolling and cutting with remaining dough.

3 Bake 9 to 12 minutes, or until golden brown around the edges and on the bottom. Cool on racks.

4 Line a large baking sheet with waxed paper. To prepare glaze, combine powdered sugar and 1½ tablespoons orange juice in

(continued on page 61)

1½ cups all-purpose flour

¾ cup yellow cornmeal

½ teaspoon baking powder

½ cup golden raisins, finely chopped

⅔ cup butter, softened

½ cup granulated sugar

⅛ teaspoon salt

⅓ cup light rum

finely grated zest of 1 large orange

1½ teaspoons vanilla extract

powdered sugar (optional)

Glaze

1½ cups powdered sugar

1½ to 2½ tablespoons orange juice or rum

about ⅓ cup nonpareils (colored sprinkles) or toasted pine nuts (optional)

Makes about 4 dozen cookies

Opposite: Sardinian Raisin-Almond Squares (page 76).
Page following: Pistachio Butter Rings (page 74).

a small bowl. Stir in enough additional orange juice to make a smooth, creamy glaze. Dip half of each cookie horizontally into glaze; set on waxed paper-lined baking sheet. Lightly sprinkle glazed half with nonpareils or pine nuts. (Dip only a few cookies at a time or glaze will set before you can sprinkle it with decorations.) Let glaze set before storing. Store in an airtight container at room temperature 1 week; freeze for longer storage.

Ginger-Rum Biscuits

(from England)

Ginger biscuits are classically English; this version sandwiches two cookies together with a decadently delicious ginger-rum buttercream. Candied or crystallized ginger can be found in most large supermarkets. I save time by mincing a whole jarful at once: Combine the ginger with about ¼ cup granulated sugar in a food processor fitted with a metal blade and pulse the machine on and off until the ginger is minced. Store in an airtight container.

1 Preheat oven to 350°F. Grease 3 large baking sheets. In a large bowl, combine flour, sugar, ginger and salt. Use a pastry blender or two knives to cut in butter until mixture resembles coarse crumbs. Add sour cream and stir to combine. Form dough into a ball; cover and refrigerate 15 minutes.

2 On a floured surface, roll dough out into a rough circle ⅛ inch thick. Cut out dough using a floured 2-inch scalloped cutter. Use a 1-inch round cutter to cut out centers of half the rounds, forming rings. Brush rings with egg glaze; sprinkle with decorating sugar. Form scraps into a ball, reroll and cut as before. Arrange rounds and rings, 1 inch apart, on prepared baking sheets.

3 Bake 8 to 11 minutes, or until pale golden on the top and golden brown on the bottom. Cool on racks.

4 To prepare buttercream, in a small mixing bowl, beat butter and ginger until creamy. Add powdered sugar ¼ cup at a time, beating well after each addition. Gradually drizzle in rum, beating until smooth and creamy.

2 cups all-purpose flour

⅔ cup granulated sugar

1½ teaspoons ground ginger

¼ teaspoon salt

½ cup cold butter, cut into 8 pieces

½ cup sour cream

1 egg white beaten with 2 teaspoons water for glaze

about ¼ cup coarse decorating sugar

Ginger-Rum Buttercream

1½ cups butter, softened

2 to 3 teaspoons minced crystallized ginger

3 cups powdered sugar

3 tablespoons light rum

Makes about 4 dozen cookies

5 Spread buttercream about ⅛ inch thick over bottoms of cookie rounds. Top with sugared cookie rings to create sandwiches; press down lightly. Store in an airtight container at room temperature 3 days, in the refrigerator 5 days. Freeze for longer storage.

Hazelnut Spirals

(Haselnuss-Schnitten, *from Austria*)

Those of you with a passion for hazelnuts (also known as filberts) will fall in love with these heavenly morsels. A spiced hazelnut filling forms a decorative spiral in a rich, lightly sweet cookie. If you wish more color contrast in the spiral, use brown sugar in the filling instead of granulated sugar.

1 In a medium bowl, combine flour, sugar, baking powder and salt. Use a pastry blender or two knives to cut in butter until mixture resembles coarse crumbs, or process in a food processor using pulses. In a small bowl, lightly beat egg and vanilla together. Add to flour mixture and stir to combine. Gather dough into a ball, wrap in waxed paper or plastic wrap and set aside at room temperature 30 minutes.

2 On a lightly floured surface, roll dough out into an 18- x 9-inch rectangle about ⅛ inch thick. (If your work surface is not large enough, roll into 2 9- x 9-inch rectangles.) If necessary, turn rectangle so that a long side is facing you. Gently spread softened butter evenly over dough. Combine remaining filling ingredients in a medium bowl. Sprinkle evenly over dough, covering all but ½ inch along the long side farthest from you. Use a rolling pin to lightly press mixture into dough. Beginning with the side closest to you, roll dough *tightly*, jelly-roll fashion. Pinch seam to seal. Wrap tightly in plastic wrap or waxed paper; refrigerate 3 hours.

3 Preheat oven to 350°F. Grease 3 to 4 large baking sheets. Use a sharp knife to cut roll into ⅜-inch slices. Arrange, 1 inch apart, on prepared baking sheets.

4 Bake 9 to 13 minutes, or until barely golden on the top and golden brown on the bottom. Cool on racks. Store in an airtight container at room temperature 1 week; freeze for longer storage.

Cookie Dough

2 cups all-purpose flour

⅓ cup granulated sugar

¼ teaspoon baking powder

⅛ teaspoon salt

½ cup + 2 tablespoons cold butter, cut into 10 pieces

1 egg

1 teaspoon vanilla extract

Filling

1 tablespoon butter, softened

¼ cup granulated sugar

¼ teaspoon ground allspice

⅛ teaspoon ground nutmeg

¾ cup ground toasted hazelnuts

Makes about 4 dozen cookies

Jumbles

(from the United States)

Recipes for these delicate sugar cookies have been around for centuries. They were extremely popular during the 1800s, comprising an amazing eight out of 21 recipes in the 1882 regional booklet, The Practical Cookbook. *Old-time jumbles (originally spelled "jumbals") were scented with rosewater, which can be found in liquor stores and some supermarkets.*

1 In a medium bowl, combine flour, baking soda and salt; set aside. In a small mixing bowl, beat butter and granulated sugar together until light and fluffy. Beat in egg yolks, sour cream and rosewater. Add flour mixture, ½ cup at a time, stirring well after each addition. Scrape dough out onto a large piece of plastic wrap; cover with the wrap. Refrigerate 8 hours or overnight.

2 Preheat oven to 325°F. Grease 3 large baking sheets. Work with ¼ of the dough at a time; refrigerate remainder. On a generously floured surface, roll dough out into a rough circle ⅛ inch thick. (Dough is very soft, so you must work quickly before it warms.) Cut out dough using a floured 2-inch cutter; reflour cutter before each use. Use a floured ½-inch cutter (or the cap from a small bottle of flavoring extract) to cut a hole in the center of each round. Gather scraps into a ball; reroll and cut. Arrange rings, 1 inch apart, on prepared baking sheets.

3 Bake 11 to 14 minutes, or until pale beige on the top and golden on the bottom. Place cookies on racks; immediately dust with powdered sugar. Cool completely. Store in an airtight container at room temperature up to 1 week; freeze for longer storage.

1⅔ cups all-purpose flour
¼ teaspoon baking soda
¼ teaspoon salt
½ cup butter, softened
¾ cup granulated sugar
2 egg yolks
3 tablespoons sour cream
2 tablespoons rosewater, or 2 tablespoons orange juice, or ½ teaspoon each vanilla extract and almond extract + 1 tablespoon milk
powdered sugar

Makes about 3½ dozen cookies

Joe Froggers

(from the United States)

*Legend tells us that these cookies were created over 100 years ago in Marble-
head, Massachusetts, by an old man called Uncle Joe. He lived alongside a frog
pond and used to trade local fishermen a batch of his favorite cookies for a jug
of their rum, which left all parties involved feeling pleased with the swap. It
was said that his cookies resembled the great, fat frogs in his pond—hence
their name. These tend to scorch if not baked on the middle oven rack, so
unless you have two ovens, only two or three of the giant cookies can be baked
at a time.*

1 In a small bowl, combine molasses and baking soda; set aside.
In a medium bowl, combine flour, ginger, nutmeg, cinnamon,
cloves, allspice and salt; set aside. In a large mixing bowl, beat
butter and sugar until combined. At low speed, gradually blend in
rum, coffee and molasses mixture. Stir in flour mixture, ½ cup at a
time, blending well after each addition. Cover bowl with plastic
wrap and refrigerate overnight, or place dough in freezer 4
hours.

2 Position rack in center of oven. Preheat oven to 350°F. Generously grease a large baking sheet (if you have two ovens, grease
two baking sheets). Place half the dough on a floured surface;
return remainder to refrigerator. Using a floured rolling pin and
working quickly, roll half the dough out into a rough circle ⅜ inch
thick. Cut out circles with a floured 5-inch round cutter (I use a
saucer and cut around it with a pointed knife). Immediately wrap
scraps and place in freezer to prevent them from becoming too soft
to work with. Use a pastry brush to brush excess flour from cut
dough. If desired, lightly sprinkle tops of cookies with chopped

1 cup dark or light unsulphured molasses
1 teaspoon baking soda
4 cups all-purpose flour
2 teaspoons ground ginger
½ teaspoon ground nutmeg
½ teaspoon ground cinnamon
½ teaspoon ground cloves
¼ teaspoon ground allspice
1 teaspoon salt
1⅓ cups butter, softened
1 cup granulated sugar
¼ cup dark or light rum, or water
¼ cup strong coffee
about 1½ cups chopped walnuts (optional)
additional granulated sugar (optional)

**Makes about 1 dozen 5-inch
cookies**

nuts and sugar. Use two large metal spatulas to place cookies, 1½ inches apart, on prepared baking sheet. Set on top of a second baking sheet for insulation.

3 Bake 9 to 13 minutes, or just until cookies spring back when lightly pressed with a fingertip; do not overbake (cookies will firm as they cool). Use two large metal spatulas or the bottom of a springform pan to transfer cookies to racks to cool.

4 While cookies are baking, continue rolling and cutting out dough, keeping remainder in refrigerator or freezer. Let cookies mellow 1 day before serving. Cut into wedges to serve. Store in an airtight container at room temperature 1 week; freeze for longer storage. If cookies become dry, put 1-2 apple wedges in the storage container with them; the cookies will soften within a day.

Lemon Cream-Filled Medallions

(Medaljakager, *from Denmark*)

A sprightly lemon filling nestles between two crisp, spicy cookies to create a celebration of flavors and textures. I imprint a design on the top cookie to create a medallion effect. Two easy ways to imprint the dough are with a textured meat tenderizer or the small holes on a box grater. Yet another way is to press a smaller cookie cutter halfway into the center of the dough.

1 To prepare cookie dough: In a medium bowl, combine flour, cinnamon, nutmeg, allspice, ginger, cloves and salt; set aside. In a large mixing bowl, beat butter, sugar and vanilla together until light and fluffy. Stir in flour mixture ½ cup at a time, blending well after each addition. Gather dough into a ball; cover and set aside 15 minutes.

2 Preheat oven to 350°F. Grease 2 to 3 large baking sheets. On a lightly floured surface, roll dough out into a rough circle a scant ⅛ inch thick. Cut out dough using a floured 2-inch cutter. Gather and reroll dough scraps. Arrange rounds, 1 inch apart, on prepared baking sheets. Imprint a design of your choice in half the rounds. Brush inprinted rounds lightly with egg glaze. If desired, sprinkle with decorating sugar.

3 Bake 10 to 13 minutes, or until golden brown. Cool on racks.

4 To prepare filling: In a small mixing bowl, blend butter, lemon zest and vanilla. Beating constantly at medium speed, add half the sugar and 2 tablespoons lemon juice. Gradually beat in remain-

2½ cups all-purpose flour
1 teaspoon ground cinnamon
½ teaspoon ground nutmeg
½ teaspoon ground allspice
½ teaspoon ground ginger
¼ teaspoon ground cloves
¼ teaspoon salt
1 cup butter, softened
¾ cup granulated sugar
1½ teaspoons vanilla extract
1 egg white beaten with 2 teaspoons water for glaze
about 2 tablespoons coarse decorating sugar
Lemon Cream Filling
3 tablespoons butter, softened
finely grated zest of 1 large lemon
1 teaspoon vanilla extract
2½ cups powdered sugar
2 to 3 tablespoons fresh lemon juice

Makes about 2½ dozen cookies

ing sugar. If necessary, add more lemon juice, a few drops at a time, to create a thick, smooth filling.

5 Spread a rounded teaspoon of filling evenly over the bottoms of the plain cookies; top with imprinted cookies. Let stand until filling sets. Store in an airtight container at room temperature 3 to 4 days, or refrigerate up to 1 week; freeze for longer storage.

New England Sour Cream Cakes

(from the United States)

A treasured old New England recipe yields this wonderfully tender cookie enriched with sour cream. Its simplicity makes it the perfect foil for numerous variations; you might try adding ½ cup golden raisins, chopped nuts or chocolate chips.

1 Preheat oven to 375°F. Grease 2 large baking sheets. In a large mixing bowl, beat butter, sugar and vanilla together until light and fluffy. Beat in egg; set aside. In a medium bowl, combine flour, baking soda, salt and nutmeg. Fold into butter mixture alternately with sour cream, ⅓ at a time. Cover and refrigerate overnight.

2 Divide dough in quarters; refrigerate all but one portion. On a floured surface, roll one quarter of dough out into a rough circle 1/4 inch thick. Cut out dough using a floured 2½-inch cutter. Gather scraps and add to next portion of dough you work on. (Quick and gentle handling is necessary as this dough softens very fast. If dough becomes too soft to work with, place in freezer for 15 minutes.) Repeat rolling and cutting until all dough is rolled out. Arrange cutouts, 1 inch apart, on prepared baking sheets.

3 Bake 6 to 9 minutes, or until golden brown around edges. While cookies are baking, prepare glaze: In a medium bowl, combine sugar and vanilla. Stir in enough milk to make a thin, smooth glaze.

4 Remove cookies from oven; immediately brush with glaze. Cool on racks.

½ cup butter, softened

1 cup granulated sugar

1 teaspoon vanilla extract

1 egg

2 cups all-purpose flour

½ teaspoon baking soda

¼ teaspoon salt

¼ teaspoon ground nutmeg

½ cup sour cream

Glaze

⅔ cup powdered sugar

½ teaspoon vanilla extract

2 to 4 teaspoons milk

Makes about 2 dozen cookies

Peanut Cakes

(Kulikuli, *from Nigeria*)

Locally grown peanuts are used deliciously in these fat, golden cookies. Street vendors sell the popular kulikuli *for nutritious midday snacks. I like them soft, but you can make this a crisp cookie by simply extending the baking time.*

1 In a medium bowl, combine flour, baking powder and salt; set aside. In a small mixing bowl, beat butter and sugar together until light and fluffy. Beat in egg and vanilla. Stir in flour mixture, ½ cup at a time, blending well after each addition. Stir in ½ cup peanuts. Form dough into a ball; cover and refrigerate 1 hour.

2 Preheat oven to 350°F. Grease 2 large baking sheets. On a lightly floured surface, roll dough out into a rough circle ¼ inch thick. Cut out dough using a floured 2½-inch cutter. Gather and reroll dough scraps. Arrange, 1 inch apart, on prepared baking sheets. Brush cookies with egg glaze and sprinkle with remaining ¼ cup peanuts.

3 Bake 10 to 11 minutes for soft cookies, 15 to 17 minutes for crisper cookies. Cool on racks. Store in an airtight container at room temperature 1 week; freeze for longer storage.

1¾ cups all-purpose flour
½ teaspoon baking powder
¼ teaspoon salt
½ cup butter, softened
¾ cup granulated sugar
1 egg
1½ teaspoons vanilla extract
¾ cup chopped unsalted peanuts
1 egg white beaten with 1 tablespoon milk for glaze

Makes about 1½ dozen cookies

Orange-Date Zebras

(from the United States)

These come from my mother, who adapted the recipe from one given to her by my father's grandmother . . . and so family traditions carry down through the generations. My contribution is the orange zest, which adds a sprightly flavor to the sweet date filling. Mom always freezes half the dough—that way, she can slice and bake it for fresh cookies in minutes! Orange-Date Zebras go wonderfully with tart orange sherbet.

1 To prepare cookie dough: In a medium bowl, combine flour, baking soda and salt; set aside. In a large mixing bowl, beat shortening, sugars and vanilla until light and fluffy. Add eggs one at a time, beating well after each addition. Stir in flour mixture ½ cup at a time, blending well after each addition. Cover dough and refrigerate 2 hours or until firm.

2 To prepare filling: In a large saucepan, combine and all filling ingredients except vanilla. Cook over low heat for 10 minutes, stirring often; mixture should be the consistency of a thick paste. Remove from heat and stir in vanilla. Let cool to room temperature. (If filling has been refrigerated, let stand at room temperature for 1 hour before using.)

3 Remove dough from refrigerator; divide in half. On a floured surface, roll half of dough out into a 9- x 14-inch rectangle, about ³⁄₁₆-inch thick. Cut a 2¼- x 14-inch strip of dough from rectangle; set aside. (This strip will become the top of your zebra "stack.") Stir date filling to loosen. Spread half the date filling over the 6¾- x 14-inch rectangle. Cut into 3 (2¼- x 14-inch) strips. Stack dough strips with date filling on top of each other, topping with plain strip. Repeat with second half of dough. Wrap both

Cookie Dough

4 cups all-purpose flour
1 teaspoon baking soda
½ teaspoon salt
1 cup shortening, softened
1 cup granulated sugar
1 cup packed brown sugar
1½ teaspoons vanilla extract
3 eggs

Date Filling

½ cup water
1 pound pitted dates, chopped
½ cup granulated sugar
grated zest of 1 large orange
1 tablespoon lemon juice
1½ teaspoons ground cinnamon
1 teaspoon vanilla extract

Makes about 8½ dozen cookies

zebra stacks in plastic wrap; refrigerate overnight. (If desired, double-wrap one of the dough logs and freeze up to 3 months. Slice frozen dough and let stand on baking sheets 10 minutes before baking.)

4 Preheat oven to 350°F. Grease 4 large baking sheets. Use a sharp knife to cut refrigerated stacks into ¼-inch slices. Arrange slices, 1 inch apart, on prepared baking sheets. Bake 8 to 11 minutes, or until golden brown. Cool on racks. Store in an airtight container at room temperature 1 week; freeze for longer storage.

Variation
Date Pinwheels: Spread each 9- x 14-inch rectangle with half the date filling, spreading to about ¼ inch from all edges. Starting with one long side, roll up tightly, jelly-roll fashion. Wrap each roll in plastic wrap; refrigerate overnight. Slice and bake as above.

Pistachio Butter Rings

(Gribee, *from Syria*)

Two ingredients make this crumbly-rich cookie unique. The first is clarified butter, which is the clear liquid fat from which the milk solids have been removed. It's a popular ingredient in Middle Eastern cooking and baking because it has a higher burning point and it keeps well without refrigeration. Semolina flour is the second unusual ingredient in this cookie. It's a high-gluten flour with a granular texture. In the West, it's most often used to make pasta.

1 Preheat oven to 300°F. Grease 4 large baking sheets. In a small mixing bowl, beat clarified butter, sugar, salt and rosewater together until light and fluffy, about 5 minutes. Stir in flours ½ cup at a time, blending well after each addition. Cover and set aside 15 minutes.

2 On a floured surface, roll dough out into a rough circle ¼ inch thick. Cut out dough using a floured 2-inch round cutter. Use a 1-inch round cutter to cut out center of circles, forming rings. Gather and reroll dough scraps. Arrange rings, 1 inch apart, on prepared baking sheets. Brush each with glaze; sprinkle with a rounded ⅛ teaspoon pistachio nuts.

3 Bake 13 to 16 minutes, or until bottoms are pale golden. Allow cookies to cool on baking sheets 2 minutes before transferring to racks to cool completely. Store in an airtight container at room temperature 1 week; freeze for longer storage.

Clarified Butter: In a small saucepan, melt 1 cup butter over low heat. When butter is melted and bubbling, remove from heat. Let stand 3 to 5 minutes. Skim off clear liquid from top; discard sediment at bottom. Makes about ⅔ cup clarified butter.

⅔ cup clarified butter, cooled to room temperature (see below)

¾ cup granulated sugar

¼ teaspoon salt

½ teaspoon rosewater

1 cup semolina flour

1 cup all-purpose flour

1 egg white beaten with 2 teaspoons water + ¼ teaspoon rosewater for glaze

about ¼ cup finely chopped pistachio nuts

Makes about 5 dozen cookies

Poppy Seed Crisps

(Ciastka Makowe, *from Poland*)

Did you know it takes 900,000 poppy seeds to equal a pound? What I'd like to know is who took the time to count all those minuscule seeds for that little bit of trivia. But what really counts is how delicious poppy seeds are in these crisp, honey-laced cookies. The seeds are soaked in a honey-orange juice mixture and, just before baking, the cookie is brushed with a honeyed egg glaze for a final soupcon of sweetness.

1 In a small saucepan, combine poppy seeds, honey and orange juice. Bring to a boil; boil 2 minutes. Remove from heat, cover and set aside 1 hour.

2 In a large bowl, combine flour, sugar and salt. Using a pastry blender or two knives, cut in butter until mixture resembles coarse crumbs, or process in a food processor using pulses. Stir in sour cream and cooled poppy seed mixture. Form dough into a ball. Wrap and refrigerate 4 hours.

3 Preheat oven to 375°F. Grease 4 large baking sheets. Divide dough in half. On a well-floured surface, roll each half out into a rough circle ⅛ inch thick. Cut out dough using a floured 2-inch cutter. Gather and reroll dough scraps. Brush cutouts with egg glaze. Arrange 1½ inches apart on prepared baking sheets.

4 Bake cookies 6 to 9 minutes, or until golden brown. Cool on racks. Store in an airtight container at room temperature 1 week; freeze for longer storage.

½ cup poppy seeds

¼ cup honey

½ cup orange juice

2 cups all-purpose flour

¾ cup powdered sugar

¼ teaspoon salt

½ cup cold butter, cut into 8 pieces

2 tablespoons sour cream

1 egg white beaten with 2 teaspoons honey for glaze

Makes about 6 dozen cookies

Sardinian Raisin-Almond Squares

(Papassinos, *from Italy*)

Scented with Marsala, these scrumptious cookies hail from Sardinia, a beautiful, mountainous island off the coast of Italy. Dry sherry can be substituted for the Marsala without any drastic change in flavor. Papassinos are bursting with raisins, candied orange peel and almonds, yet the cookie around them stays buttery-crisp.

1 In a small bowl, combine Marsala, raisins and orange peel. Cover and set aside overnight. (Or cover and microwave at full power 30 seconds; let stand 5 minutes.)

2 In a small mixing bowl, beat butter, sugar and salt together until light and fluffy. Beat in egg. Stir in fruit with Marsala. Add flour ½ cup at a time, blending well after addition. Stir in nuts. Cover bowl and refrigerate dough overnight, or cover and place in freezer 4 hours.

3 Preheat oven to 325°F. Divide dough in half; return one half to refrigerator. On a well-floured surface, roll half the dough out to a 10½- x 6-inch rectangle about ⅜ inch thick. Using a large, floured knife, cut dough into 28 (1½-inch) squares, cutting 4 strips one way and 7 strips the other way. Arrange, 1 inch apart, on a large ungreased baking sheet. Repeat rolling and cutting with remaining dough and second baking sheet.

4 Bake 18 to 22 minutes, or until golden brown around the edges.

(continued on page 77)

⅓ cup Marsala
¾ cup golden raisins
⅓ cup candied orange peel
½ cup butter, softened
⅔ cup granulated sugar
¼ teaspoon salt
1 egg
1½ cups all-purpose flour
1¼ cups chopped toasted almonds
Orange Glaze
⅔ cup powdered sugar
1½ to 2 tablespoons orange juice

Makes about 4½ dozen cookies

Opposite: Almond Sighs (page 148), Chocolate Coconut Macaroons (page 89), and Peanut Butter Rebels (page 98). Page following: Chinese Almond Cookies (page 112).

5 While cookies are baking, prepare glaze: In a small bowl, combine powdered sugar with 1½ tablespoons orange juice, stirring until smooth. If necessary, add more orange juice to make a thin, smooth glaze. Brush glaze over hot cookies while still on baking sheets. Cool on racks. Store in an airtight container at room temperature 1 week; freeze for longer storage.

Opposite: Danish Dandies (page 117).
Page preceding: Colombian Coffee Cookies
  (page 116).

Parson's Hats

(Pfaffenhütchen, *from Germany*)

Shaped like a tricornered clergyman's hat, these tender cookies enfold a "heavenly" hazelnut-orange filling. The chopped, packaged hazelnuts that can now be found in most large supermarkets end the hassle of removing the skins from whole hazelnuts. If you can't find chopped hazelnuts, see page 19 for instructions on how to blanch the nuts for this filling.

1 In a small mixing bowl, beat butter, sugar and salt together until light and fluffy. Beat in egg and vanilla. Stir in flour ½ cup at a time, blending well after each addition. Stir in nuts. Form dough into a ball; cover and set aside 10 minutes.

2 Preheat oven to 375°F. Grease 2 large baking sheets. To prepare filling: In a medium bowl, combine hazelnuts, sugar, salt and orange zest. Stir in enough orange juice to make a soft but thick paste; set aside.

3 On a floured surface, roll dough out into a rough circle ⅛ inch thick. Cut out dough using a floured, 3-inch scalloped cutter. Gather and reroll dough scraps. *Lightly* brush rounds with egg glaze. Place a rounded half-teaspoonful of filling in the center of each round. Pull edges up so that circle forms three sides; pinch seams together to form a pyramid. Brush with egg glaze and sprinkle with decorating sugar. Arrange, 1 inch apart, on prepared baking sheets.

4 Bake 11 to 15 minutes, or until pale golden brown. Cool on racks. Store in an airtight container at room temperature 4 to 5 days; freeze for longer storage.

Cookie

⅔ cup butter, softened
½ cup granulated sugar
⅛ teaspoon salt
1 egg
1 teaspoon vanilla extract
2¼ cups all-purpose flour
⅓ cup finely ground hazelnuts
1 egg white beaten with 2 teaspoons water for glaze
about 2 tablespoons coarse decorating sugar

Hazelnut-Orange Filling

¾ cup coarsely ground hazelnuts
½ cup granulated sugar
pinch of salt
2 teaspoons finely grated orange zest
2 to 3 tablespoons orange juice

Makes about 3 dozen cookies

DROP COOKIES

Next to bar cookies, drop cookies are the quickest and easiest to make. They're also extremely versatile, and can be as simple or sophisticated as your whim or the occasion dictates. Drop cookies are easy to double-batch and freeze well, so you can always have a cookie jar full of delicious temptation!

Drop cookies are made by using a spoon to drop blobs of a rather soft dough onto a baking sheet. It's important to use the right kind of spoon. The "teaspoon" and "tablespoon" used to drop the dough refers to regular flatware, not measuring spoons. Another spoon or small rubber spatula can be used to push the dough off the dropping spoon onto the baking sheet. I find it easier to use my finger as a pusher (which also allows for licks!).

Customize your drop cookies by making them as large or small as you wish. Make sure you leave an adequate amount of space between the cookies to allow for spreading. Extra-large cookies (2 heaping tablespoons of dough) will require about 2 inches between cookies; soft doughs will spread more than firm ones. When changing the size of a cookie, use your common sense to adjust the baking time (less for smaller, more for larger cookies).

Two British cookies in this chapter—*Queen's Cakes* and *Irish Whiskey Seed Cakes*—depart from the drop cookie norm in that the dough is dropped into miniature muffin tins instead of onto baking sheets. The results are tiny, tender-crisp cookies that are pretty and delicious enough to serve to your best company.

Italian Almond Florentines

It takes Herculean willpower to resist these chewy, candylike cookies coated with chocolate. Because of their name, Florentines are thought to have originated in Florence, but Austrian bakers also claim to have invented them. The cookies are made by combining a boiling syrup made of honey, sugar and cream with fruits and nuts. A few minutes in the oven and this molten mixture transforms into an absolutely irresistible cookie!

1 Preheat oven to 350°F. Grease and flour 4 large baking sheets. In a heavy medium saucepan, combine butter, sugar, cream and honey. Cook over low heat, stirring occasionally, until butter melts. Increase heat to medium-high and bring mixture to a boil, stirring frequently. Remove from heat; stir in fruit, flour and almonds.

2 Drop batter by rounded teaspoons, 3 inches apart, on prepared baking sheets. Use back of spoon to spread each mound of batter into a thin circle about 2½ inches in diameter, making them as round as possible.

3 Bake 10 to 13 minutes, or until edges are golden brown; centers of cookies will still be bubbling. Let cool on baking sheets 3 minutes. Using a metal spatula, transfer cookies to racks to cool completely.

⅓ cup butter

⅔ cup granulated sugar

½ cup whipping cream

2 tablespoons honey

¼ cup candied orange peel, finely chopped

¼ cup candied cherries, rinsed in hot water, thoroughly drained and finely chopped

⅓ cup all-purpose flour

1⅔ cups sliced blanched almonds

Chocolate Glaze

5 ounces semisweet chocolate

2 tablespoons extra-strong coffee

3 tablespoons butter

Makes about 4 dozen cookies

4 To prepare glaze: Combine all ingredients in the top of a double boiler over simmering water. Heat, stirring occasionally, until mixture is smooth, about 5 minutes. Remove from heat. Cool 10 minutes, stirring occasionally. Or combine all ingredients in a medium bowl. Microwave at 50% power 1½ minutes. Remove from microwave oven and stir until smooth.

5 Line a large baking sheet with waxed paper. Turn cooled cookies upside down on the paper. Use the back of a teaspoon to spread chocolate over flat side of each cookie. If you wish a decorative finish, refrigerate cookies about 5 minutes, or until chocolate is firm but not set. Use a cake decorating comb or fork to make wavy lines in surface of chocolate; refrigerate until chocolate is set. Store cookies in an airtight container in the refrigerator 1 week.

Anzac Crisps

(from Australia)

The name Anzac comes from the nickname given to World War I soldiers in the Australian and New Zealand Army Corps. This easy oatmeal-coconut drop cookie is lightly flavored with golden syrup, a special sweetener made from evaporated sugar cane juice. Golden syrup—the best-known brand being Lyle's—is found in the gourmet section of most large supermarkets. Honey can be substituted, but nothing quite matches the rich, nutty flavor of golden syrup.

1 Preheat oven to 325°F. Grease 3 large baking sheets. In a large bowl, combine oats, flour, sugar, coconut, baking soda and salt; set aside. In a small saucepan, combine butter and golden syrup. Place over medium heat, stirring occasionally, until butter is melted. Pour into flour mixture; stir to combine.

2 Gather dough by well-rounded teaspoons; it is very crumbly, so you will need to use your fingers to lightly pack dough into the spoon. Invert mounds of dough, 1½ inches apart, on prepared baking sheets, shaping with your fingers if necessary.

3 Bake 10 to 13 minutes, or until deep golden brown. Remove cookies from oven; let stand on baking sheets 3 minutes. Cool on racks. Store in an airtight container at room temperature 1 week; freeze for longer storage.

1 cup rolled oats
1 cup all-purpose flour
⅔ cup granulated sugar
1 cup grated or flaked coconut
1 teaspoon baking soda
⅛ teaspoon salt
½ cup butter
3 tablespoons Lyle's golden syrup

Makes about 3 dozen cookies

Apricot Oaties

(from Scotland)

In Samuel Johnson's 1755 Dictionary of the English Language, the definition of oats was: "A grain which in England is generally given to horses, but which in Scotland supports the people." Of course now we know the canny Scots knew very well what they were doing all along! A full cup of apricot jam goes right into this dough, with a dollop added to the top of each cookie. Be sure to use a good-quality apricot jam; it should be thick in order for the dough not to become too soft.

1 Preheat oven to 350°F. Grease 4 large baking sheets. In a medium bowl, combine oats, flour, cinnamon, nutmeg, baking soda, baking powder and salt; set aside. In a large mixing bowl, beat butter, sugar and vanilla until light and fluffy. Add 1 cup jam, then eggs, one at a time, beating well after each addition. Stir in flour mixture ½ cup at a time, blending well after each addition. Stir in nuts. Drop dough by rounded tablespoons, 1½ inches apart, on prepared baking sheets. Use the tip of a wooden spoon handle to make an indentation in the center of each cookie; do not press all the way to the baking sheet, or the jam will seep through the bottom of the cookie. Fill each indentation with about ¼ teaspoon of the additional ⅔ cup jam.

2 Bake 10 to 13 minutes, or until golden brown. Let cookies stand on baking sheets 2 minutes before removing to racks to cool. Store in an airtight container at room temperature 1 week; freeze for longer storage. Place a sheet of waxed paper between layers to store.

Ingredients
2½ cups rolled oats
2½ cups all-purpose flour
1½ teaspoons ground cinnamon
½ teaspoon ground nutmeg
1 teaspoon baking soda
½ teaspoon baking powder
½ teaspoon salt
1 cup butter, softened
1½ cups granulated sugar
2 teaspoons vanilla extract
about 1⅔ cups thick apricot jam
2 eggs
1½ cups chopped toasted walnuts

Makes about 7 dozen cookies

Bert's Benne Wafers

(from the United States)

My dear friend Bert Greene shared this wonderful heritage recipe with me, and it's become one of my favorites. I've added a soupcon of orange zest, which I think goes nicely with the flavor of sesame. Benne (pronounced benny) is an old Southern name for sesame seed, which is said to have originally come to North America on slave ships. Legend has it that eating Benne Wafers brings good fortune. Happy eating and good luck!

1 Preheat oven to 400°F. Line as many large baking sheets as you have with foil; butter foil. (Depending on the size of the baking sheet, only 6 to 8 cookies can be baked on one sheet at a time. To reuse sheets, let cool and cover with new buttered foil.)

2 In a small mixing bowl, beat egg, vanilla and salt to combine. Add butter, brown sugar, flour and orange zest; beat at medium speed until smooth. Stir in pecans and sesame seed.

3 Drop batter by heaping teaspoons at least 3 inches apart on prepared baking sheets. These cookies spread a great deal and need plenty of room to do so. Only bake 6 to 8 cookies on each baking sheet (depending on size of sheet).

4 Bake 5 to 7 minutes, or until cookies are golden brown on top and browned around the edges. Switch baking sheets from top to bottom and front to back after 3 minutes baking time. Slide foil off baking sheet. Leave cookies on foil; place on racks until completely cool. Peel foil away from cooled cookies. Repeat baking on foil-lined sheets until all batter is used. Store in an airtight container at room temperature 1 week; freeze for longer storage. Benne Wafers will become sticky if storage container isn't absolutely airtight.

1 egg

½ teaspoon vanilla extract

⅛ teaspoon salt

6 tablespoons butter, melted

¾ cup packed brown sugar

¼ cup all-purpose flour

2 teaspoons finely grated orange zest

½ cup toasted chopped pecans

½ cup toasted sesame seed

Makes about 3 dozen cookies

Bolivian Almond Cookies

(Alfajores de Almendras)

Crisp on the edges and semisoft in the center, these quick drop cookies are the perfect partner for ice cream or sherbet. They use ground and sliced almonds—plus almond extract—for a triple-almond flavor punch. You can easily grind almonds in a food processor using a metal blade in quick on/off pulses. Or use a blender and grind the almonds in ½-cup batches. Be sure toasted nuts are completely cool before you grind them.

1 Preheat oven to 350°F. Grease 2 to 3 large baking sheets. In a medium bowl, combine flour, ground almonds and salt; set aside. In a large mixing bowl, beat butter, sugar and extracts until light and fluffy. Beat in eggs. Stir in lemon zest and flour mixture ½ cup at a time, blending well after each addition. Drop dough by rounded tablespoons, 1½ inches apart, on prepared baking sheets. Flatten slightly with the back of a spoon; sprinkle with sliced almonds.

2 Bake 10 to 13 minutes, or until edges are golden brown. Cool on racks. Store in an airtight container at room temperature 1 week; freeze for longer storage.

1¼ cups all-purpose flour
2 cups ground toasted almonds
¼ teaspoon salt
1 cup butter, softened
1 cup granulated sugar
1 teaspoon vanilla extract
¾ teaspoon almond extract
2 eggs
finely grated zest of 1 large lemon
about 1 cup sliced almonds

Makes about 3½ dozen cookies

Brazil Nut Wafers

(Biscoito de Renda Brasileira, *from Brazil*)

Brazil is South America's largest producer of coffee and cocoa, and this lacy cookie uses those flavors as enhancements to a Brazil nut base. Beginning as a batter—rather than a dough—it transforms from a "blob" on the baking sheet to a molten, lacy creation. The cookie crisps as it cools to form a sweet, crunchy wafer.

1 Preheat oven to 325°F. Grease 4 large baking sheets. In a large bowl, combine flour, cocoa, sugars and cinnamon. Stir in butter and coffee, then nuts.

2 Drop batter by rounded teaspoons 3 inches apart on prepared baking sheets.

3 Bake 11 to 14 minutes, or until cookie feels firm when lightly pressed with your fingertip. Let cookies stand on baking sheets 45 seconds to firm. Transfer to racks to cool. If cookies begin to stick to baking sheets while you're removing them, return the sheet to the oven for 1 minute. Store cookies in an airtight container at room temperature 1 week; freeze for longer storage. These cookies are very fragile, so it is best to store them in single layers.

¾ *cup all-purpose flour*
¼ *cup unsweetened cocoa powder*
½ *cup packed brown sugar*
½ *cup granulated sugar*
¾ *teaspoon ground cinnamon*
½ *cup butter, melted*
2 *tablespoons very strong coffee*
1 *cup finely chopped Brazil nuts*

Makes about 3½ dozen cookies

Butter Drops

(from the United States)

Butter Drops are the "mother" of the famous Toll House Cookie. Recipes for Butter Drops appear in dozens of old cookbooks, beginning with American Cookery *by Amelia Simmons. The chocolate chip cookie was created by Ruth Wakefield, who ran the Toll House Restaurant in Massachusetts. Mrs. Wakefield, in a moment of brilliant inspiration, cut up bars of chocolate to add to the Butter Drop dough—and in one brief, shining moment, history was made. That recipe is included here for your pleasure (see variations). And, speaking of pleasure, try using macadamia nuts in your chocolate chip cookies . . . pure heaven!*

1 Preheat oven to 375°F. Grease 4 large baking sheets. In a medium bowl, combine flour, baking soda and salt; set aside. In a large mixing bowl, beat butter and sugars together until light and fluffy. Beat in eggs and vanilla. Stir in flour mixture, ½ cup at a time, blending well after each addition.

2 Drop dough by well rounded teaspoons 2 inches apart on prepared baking sheets.

3 Bake 6 to 10 minutes, or until lightly browned. (A 6- to 7-minute baking time will produce soft cookies; 8 to 10 minutes produces crisp cookies.) Cool on racks. Store in an airtight container at room temperature 1 week; freeze for longer storage.

Variations

Classic Toll House Chocolate Chip Cookies: Stir 1 12-ounce package semisweet chocolate chips (2 cups) and 1 cup chopped nuts into final dough mixture. Makes about 7 dozen cookies.

Decadent Chocolate Chunk Cookies: Cut 1 pound semisweet bar chocolate into ⅜- to ½-inch chunks; stir into final dough mixture. Some supermarkets carry packaged "chocolate chunks."

2¼ cups all-purpose flour

1 teaspoon baking soda

1 teaspoon salt

1 cup butter, softened

¾ cup granulated sugar

¾ cup packed brown sugar

2 eggs

1 teaspoon vanilla extract

Makes about 6 dozen 2-inch cookies

Cherry-Coconut Macaroons

(from the United States)

Coconuts—the fruit of the coconut palm—take a full year to develop. One taste of these rich, chewy cookies and I think you'll agree it's worth the wait! The cherries add extra softness, but be sure to squeeze as much juice as possible from the cherries—too much liquid and the batter will spread while baking, giving you funny, "hat-shaped" macaroons.

1 Place chopped cherries in a strainer and press with the back of a spoon to extract as much juice as possible. Place cherries on a double thickness of paper towel; wring and squeeze paper towel to extract more juice. Spread cherries on another sheet of paper towel until ready to use.

2 Preheat oven to 325°F. Grease 3 to 4 large baking sheets. In a large mixing bowl, beat eggs and salt until light. Beating constantly at medium speed, add sugar ¼ cup at a time, beating well after each addition. Increase speed to high; continue beating until mixture is thick and pale and ribbons form in bowl when beaters are lifted, 5 to 10 minutes. Fold in vanilla and flour, then coconut and the chopped cherries. Drop dough by rounded tablespoons, 1½ inches apart, on prepared baking sheets. If desired, place a maraschino cherry quarter in the center of each cookie; press down lightly.

3 Bake 15 to 19 minutes, or until golden brown on the tips. Cool on racks. Store in an airtight container at room temperature 2 weeks; freeze for longer storage.

½ cup finely chopped maraschino cherries

2 eggs

⅛ teaspoon salt

¾ cup granulated sugar

2 teaspoons vanilla extract

⅓ cup all-purpose flour

2 cups flaked coconut

about 9 whole maraschino cherries, quartered and blotted thoroughly on paper towel (optional)

Makes about 3 dozen cookies

Variations

Chocolate-Cherry-Coconut Macaroons: Add 1 package (6 ounces) semisweet chocolate chips.

Chocolate Chip-Coconut Macaroons: Substitute 1 package (6 ounces) semisweet chocolate chips for the chopped maraschino cherries.

Chocolate-Coconut Macaroons: Omit cherries. Fold in 2 ounces melted unsweetened chocolate with the flour. If desired, add 1 cup *miniature* semisweet chocolate chips.

Nutty Coconut Macaroons: Substitute 1 cup chopped toasted nuts for the chopped maraschino cherries. Before baking, top macaroons with a nut half.

Honeyed Whole Wheat–Granola Cookies

(from the United States)

What a delicious way to get a little nutrition into your favorite cookie monster! Whole wheat flour, toasted wheat germ and granola add flavor and fiber to these delicious, crispy cookies. You can either buy the wheat germ already toasted or toast it yourself in a dry skillet over medium heat just until lightly browned. Sunflower seeds or chocolate chips (see variations) can be added to suit your pleasure!

1 Preheat oven to 350°F. Grease 4 large baking sheets. In a medium bowl, combine granola, flour, wheat germ, baking soda, cinnamon, nutmeg and salt; set aside. In a large mixing bowl, beat butter, brown sugar and vanilla until light and fluffy. Beat in honey and orange zest. Stir in flour mixture ½ cup at a time, blending well after each addition. Stir in raisins and nuts. Drop dough by heaping tablespoons, 1½ inches apart, on prepared baking sheets.

2 Bake 6 to 10 minutes, or until brown around the edges. Six-minute cookies will be soft; 8- to 10-minute cookies, crisp. Cool on baking sheet 3 minutes before transferring to racks to cool completely. Store in an airtight container at room temperature 1 week; freeze for longer storage.

Variations

Granola-Sunflower Seed Cookies: Substitute 1 cup toasted, unsalted sunflower seeds for 1 cup nuts.

Granola-Chocolate Chip Cookies: Substitute 1 cup semisweet chocolate chips for either the raisins or the nuts.

2 cups regular granola
1¼ cups whole wheat flour
⅓ cup toasted wheat germ
1 teaspoon baking soda
¾ teaspoon ground cinnamon
½ teaspoon ground nutmeg
½ teaspoon salt
1 cup butter, softened
1 cup packed brown sugar
1½ teaspoons vanilla extract
⅓ cup honey
grated zest of 1 medium orange
1 cup dark raisins
1 cup chopped toasted almonds, pecans or walnuts

Makes about 5 dozen cookies

Irish Whiskey–Seed Cakes

Like my grandmother's Irish soda bread, these tiny gems are studded with currants and caraway seeds and lightly scented with Irish whiskey. Put a twinkle in anyone's eye by serving these cookies with Irish coffee—a heady concoction of strong coffee fortified with a healthy splash of Irish whiskey, and topped with a dollop of gently whipped cream. 'Tis enough to make a strong man swoon with pleasure!

1 Preheat oven to 350°F. Grease 36 miniature (1¾- x ¾-inch) muffin tins; set aside. In a medium bowl, combine flour, baking soda, caraway seeds and salt; set aside. In a large mixing bowl, beat butter, sugar and orange zest together until light and fluffy. Beat in whiskey 1 tablespoon at a time. Stir in flour mixture ½ cup at a time, blending well after each addition. Stir in currants. Divide batter evenly among prepared muffin tins (about 1 heaping tablespoon each).

2 Bake cookies about 30 minutes, or until crisp and pale golden brown. Meanwhile, prepare glaze: In a small bowl, combine sugar and milk. Add enough whiskey to make a thin, creamy glaze.

3 Transfer cookies from tins to a rack. Brush glaze over warm cookies. Cool to room temperature on racks. Store in an air-tight container at room temperature 1 week; freeze for longer storage.

2 cups all-purpose flour
½ teaspoon baking soda
1 teaspoon caraway seeds, chopped
¼ teaspoon salt
1 cup butter, softened
½ cup granulated sugar
finely grated zest of 1 small orange
⅓ cup Irish or other whiskey
¼ cup dried currants
Irish Whiskey Glaze
½ cup powdered sugar
1½ teaspoons milk
1 tablespoon Irish whiskey

Makes 3 dozen cookies

Molasses-Coconut Cookies

(Masitas de Chancaca, *from Chile*)

Semisoft and chewy, these cookies are the perfect partner for an icy glass of milk. Chileans use chancaca, *a crude native molasses, in this dough. Since most palates prefer a more refined flavor, I've substituted light unsulphured molasses. Don't be put off by the lard—it gives the cookies a lovely nutty taste. If you simply don't want to use it, substitute shortening or unsalted butter.*

1 Preheat oven to 375°F. Grease 3 large baking sheets. In a medium bowl, combine flour, ginger, baking soda and salt; set aside. In a large mixing bowl, beat lard and sugar until light and fluffy. Gradually beat in molasses. Add eggs; beat to combine. Stir in flour mixture ½ cup at a time, blending well after each addition. Stir in coconut. Drop dough by rounded tablespoons, 1½ inches apart, on prepared baking sheets.

2 Bake 8 to 11 minutes, or until golden brown; cookies will be soft. Cool on racks. Store in an airtight container at room temperature 1 week; freeze for longer storage.

2 cups all-purpose flour
2 teaspoons ground ginger
½ teaspoon baking soda
½ teaspoon salt
¾ cup lard or shortening, softened
¾ cup granulated sugar
½ cup light unsulphured molasses
2 eggs
1 cup flaked or shredded coconut

Makes about 4 dozen cookies

Opposite: Georgetown Lime Cookies (page 121).
Page following: Macaroon Jam Slices (page 126).

Oatmeal Florentines

(Florentýnky Z Ovesných Vlŏvcek, *from Czechoslovakia*)

Crisp and buttery, these easy, elegant cookies are a dream . . . both in the making and in the eating! The secret to their nutty flavor is browning the oats in butter before they're added to the batter. If you want to gild the lily, dip these heavenly crisps halfway into melted chocolate.

1 In a large skillet, melt ¼ cup butter. Add oats and cook over medium heat, stirring frequently, until oats are golden brown. Cool to room temperature.

2 Preheat oven to 350°F. Generously grease and flour 3 to 4 large baking sheets. In a small saucepan, melt remaining ¼ cup butter. Pour into a medium bowl and stir in all remaining ingredients except chocolate. Drop level tablespoons of batter, 2 inches apart, on prepared baking sheets.

3 Bake 8 to 9 minutes, or until golden brown. Using a metal spatula, quickly remove cookies from baking sheets. Handle gently; they're very fragile. Cool on racks.

4 If you wish to dip the Florentines in chocolate, line a baking sheet with waxed paper. Place melted chocolate in a small, deep bowl. Dip half of each cookie into chocolate and shake gently to remove excess. Place on waxed paper-lined baking sheet until chocolate is set. Store in an airtight container at room temperature 3 to 4 days; freeze for longer storage.

½ cup butter
1½ cups rolled oats
1 tablespoon all-purpose flour
⅔ cup granulated sugar
1 teaspoon baking powder
¼ teaspoon ground cinnamon
1 egg, lightly beaten
1 teaspoon vanilla extract
6 to 8 ounces semisweet chocolate, melted and warm (optional)

Makes about 3½ dozen cookies

Opposite: Pistachio Jam Cookies (page 136), Melting Moments (page 127).
Page preceding: Peanut Butter 'n Jellies (page 132).

Old-Fashioned Oatmeal Cookies

(from the United States)

This chameleon-like cookie can change its delicious character with the addition of coconut, dried fruit, chocolate chips, raisins, nuts, cocoa . . . almost anything your heart desires!

1 Preheat oven to 350°F. Grease 2 large baking sheets. In a medium bowl, combine oats, flour, baking powder, cinnamon, nutmeg and salt; set aside. In large mixing bowl, beat butter, brown sugar and vanilla together until light and fluffy. Add eggs one at a time, beating well after each addition. Stir in flour mixture, ½ cup at a time, blending well after each addition. Stir in nuts and raisins. Drop dough by heaping tablespoons, 1½ inches apart, on prepared baking sheets.

2 Bake 9 to 13 minutes, or until golden brown. Let stand on baking sheets 2 minutes before transferring to racks to cool. Store in an airtight container at room temperature 10 days; freeze for longer storage.

Variations

Coconut-Oatmeal Cookies: Omit raisins; nuts are optional. Add 1 cup shredded or flaked coconut to final dough.

Oatmeal-Brownie Drops: Add ½ cup unsweetened cocoa powder to flour mixture; increase sugar to 2 cups. Substitute one cup semi-sweet chocolate chips for the raisins. Bake 9 minutes; let stand on baking sheets 2 minutes. Cookies will be soft.

---

2 cups rolled oats

1½ cups all-purpose flour

1 teaspoon baking powder

1 teaspoon ground cinnamon

½ teaspoon ground nutmeg

½ teaspoon salt

1 cup butter, softened

1½ cups packed brown sugar

2 teaspoons vanilla extract

2 eggs

1 cup chopped toasted walnuts

1 cup raisins

Makes about 5 dozen cookies

Mocha-Oatmeal Cookies: Prepare *Oatmeal-Brownie Drops*, adding 2 tablespoons instant coffee *powder* to butter mixture. Beat a full 2 minutes before adding eggs.

Fruited Oatmeal Cookies: Substitute 2 cups mixed chopped dried fruits of your choice (apricots, prunes, apples, peaches) for 1 cup raisins. The 1 cup nuts is optional. Unless dried fruit is soft, rehydrate by placing fruit in a bowl and mixing with 2 cups boiling water. Let stand 15 minutes; drain and blot dry on paper towels before using.

Chocolate Chip-Oatmeal Cookies: Substitute 1½ cups semisweet chocolate chips for 1 cup raisins.

Brown Sugar Drops

(from the United States)

My great-grandmother Tyler handwrote all her favorite recipes in clothbound notebooks, creating a mouthwatering history of Tyler meals in the early 1900s. Here, one of her heirloom recipes uses dark brown sugar and buttermilk for soul-satisfying, old-fashioned flavor. It also calls for shortening which, in those times of scarce refrigeration, was often used because it could be kept longer than butter without going rancid.

1 Preheat oven to 375°F. Grease 3 to 4 large baking sheets. In a medium bowl, combine flour, cream of tartar, baking soda and salt; set aside. In a large mixing bowl, beat shortening, brown sugar and vanilla until well combined. Add eggs one at a time, then buttermilk, beating well after each addition. Stir in flour mixture ½ cup at a time, blending well after each addition. Drop dough by rounded tablespoons, 1½ inches apart, on prepared baking sheets. Lightly press a pecan half into top of each cookie.

2 Bake 8 to 11 minutes, or until golden brown on the bottom. Cool on racks. Store in an airtight container at room temperature 1 week; freeze for longer storage.

Variation
Spicy Brown Sugar Drops: Add 1 teaspoon ground cinnamon and ½ teaspoon each ground allspice and nutmeg to the dry ingredients.

3½ cups all-purpose flour

2 teaspoons cream of tartar

½ teaspoon baking soda

½ teaspoon salt

1 cup shortening, softened

2 cups packed dark brown sugar

1 teaspoon vanilla extract

2 eggs

¼ cup buttermilk

about 65 pecan halves

Makes about 5½ dozen cookies

Parkin Drops

(from Canada)

This popular Nova Scotian cookie has its roots in the British Isles. The oats give Parkin Drops a delightful chewy texture and the dark corn syrup adds a toasty flavor. These cookies spread out when they're baked, but their delicious taste makes up for what they lack in beauty.

1 Preheat oven to 350°F. Grease and flour 3 large baking sheets. In a medium saucepan over medium heat, stir corn syrup and butter until butter melts. Remove from heat. Stir in brown sugar and milk; set aside 10 minutes. In a large bowl, combine oats, flour, baking powder and ginger. Stir in syrup mixture. Drop dough by rounded teaspoons, 2 inches apart, on prepared baking sheets.

2 Bake 9 to 13 minutes, or until deep golden brown. Cool on racks. Store in an airtight container at room temperature 1 week; freeze for longer storage.

1 cup dark corn syrup
1/3 cup butter
1/3 cup packed brown sugar
3 tablespoons milk
2 cups rolled oats
1 cup all-purpose flour
1 teaspoon baking powder
1 teaspoon ground ginger

Makes about 3 dozen cookies

Peanut Butter Rebels

(from the United States)

Called "rebels" because, unlike the classic crisp peanut butter cookies, these are delectably soft. Contributing to that softness is maple syrup, which I discovered long ago is a congenial companion to peanut butter. My very first apartment was shared with three girls from Wisconsin whose favorite breakfast consisted of two slices of toast spread with peanut butter and drizzled with maple syrup. I soon fell into their eccentric habit and have been a dedicated fan of that delicious duo ever since!

1 Preheat oven to 350°F. Grease 4 large baking sheets. In a medium bowl, combine flour, baking powder, baking soda, cinnamon, nutmeg and salt; set aside. In a large mixing bowl, beat peanut butter, cream cheese, brown sugar and vanilla until light and fluffy. Gradually beat in maple syrup. Stir in flour mixture ½ cup at a time, blending well after each addition. Drop heaping tablespoons of dough, 1½ inches apart, on prepared baking sheets. Sprinkle with chopped peanuts.

2 Bake 9 to 12 minutes, or until golden brown on the bottom; cookies should be soft. Cool on racks. Store in an airtight container at room temperature 1 week; freeze for longer storage.

2¾ cups all-purpose flour
1½ teaspoons baking powder
½ teaspoon baking soda
¾ teaspoon ground cinnamon
½ teaspoon ground nutmeg
¼ teaspoon salt
1 cup chunky peanut butter
8 ounces cream cheese, softened
⅔ cup packed brown sugar
1½ teaspoons vanilla extract
1 cup maple syrup
about ½ cup chopped unsalted peanuts

Makes about 6 dozen cookies

Piña Colada Drops

(from Jamaica)

Redolent of rum, these drop cookies are reminiscent of the popular Caribbean pineapple-coconut drink. It's important to squeeze as much juice as possible from the pineapple in order for the batter not to become too moist.

1 Preheat oven to 375°F. Grease 4 large baking sheets. In a medium bowl, combine flour, baking soda and salt; set aside. Turn pineapple into a strainer set over a small bowl. Use your fingers or the back of a tablespoon to firmly press pineapple into strainer, extracting as much juice as possible. Set aside pineapple and juice. In a large mixing bowl, beat butter, sugars and vanilla until light and fluffy. Beat in egg. Stir in rum alternately with flour mixture, 1/3 at a time, blending well after each addition. Stir in coconut and reserved pineapple. Drop dough by rounded tablespoons, 1½ inches apart, on prepared baking sheets.

2 Bake 8 to 11 minutes, or until top springs back when lightly pressed with a fingertip.

3 While cookies are baking, prepare glaze: In a medium bowl, combine powdered sugar, rum and vanilla. Add enough pineapple juice to make a smooth and creamy glaze of medium consistency. Brush glaze over hot cookies while still on baking sheets. Transfer cookies to racks to cool. Store in an airtight container at room temperature 1 week; freeze for longer storage.

Variation
Nutty Piña Colada Drops: Add 1 cup chopped pecans or walnuts with coconut.

3 cups all-purpose flour
1 teaspoon baking soda
½ teaspoon salt
1 can (8¼ ounces) juice-pack crushed pineapple
1 cup butter, softened
½ cup packed brown sugar
½ cup granulated sugar
½ teaspoon vanilla extract
1 egg
½ cup dark or light rum
1 cup flaked coconut
Pineapple-Rum Glaze
1¼ cups powdered sugar
1 tablespoon dark or light rum
½ teaspoon vanilla extract
1 to 2 tablespoons pineapple juice

Makes about 5 dozen cookies

Praline Kisses

(from the United States)

This incredibly quick and easy recipe is the kind every cook needs for drop-in guests or last-minute company. Praline Kisses have the taste and texture of the famous Southern praline candy without the bother of lengthy cooking on top of the stove. Pecans are traditional, but walnuts, cashews or even macadamia nuts make delicious substitutions.

1 Preheat oven to 325°F. Grease 3 large baking sheets. In a small mixing bowl, beat egg white and salt at medium speed until soft peaks form. Increase speed to medium-high and add sugar a tablespoon at a time, beating until all the sugar is incorporated (mixture will be thick). Stir in flour, cinnamon, vanilla and nuts. Drop mixture by level teaspoons, 1½ inches apart, on prepared baking sheets.

2 Bake 10 to 13 minutes, or until dry and firm on the top. Cool 1 minute on baking sheets. Transfer to racks to cool completely. Store in an airtight container at room temperature 10 days; freeze for longer storage.

1 egg white, room temperature

⅛ teaspoon salt

1 cup packed brown sugar

1 tablespoon all-purpose flour

⅛ teaspoon cinnamon

1 teaspoon vanilla extract

1½ cups chopped toasted pecans

Makes about 3½ dozen cookies

Queen's Cakes

(from England)

Though rich with sour cream, cherries and currants, Queen's Cakes somehow retain their lightness. A delicious paradox, they're crisp on the outside and tender inside. If you don't have currants, finely chopped raisins—golden or dark—may be substituted. Serve these miniature sweets with steaming-hot cups of coffee or tea and everyone will shout, "Long live the Queen!"

1 Preheat oven to 375°F. Grease 36 miniature (1¾- x ¾-inch) muffin tins. In a medium bowl, combine flour, baking soda and salt; set aside. In a large mixing bowl, beat butter, sugar and extracts together until light and fluffy. Gradually beat in sour cream. Stir in flour mixture ½ cup at a time, blending well after each addition. Stir in currants and cherries. Spoon into prepared tins, filling almost full. Sprinkle lightly with decorating sugar.

2 Bake cakes 18 to 22 minutes, or until golden brown. Remove from tins and cool on racks. Store in an airtight container at room temperature 3 to 4 days; freeze for longer storage.

2 cups all-purpose flour

¼ teaspoon baking soda

¼ teaspoon salt

⅔ cup butter, softened

⅔ cup granulated sugar

1 teaspoon vanilla extract

¼ teaspoon almond extract

⅔ cup sour cream

½ cup dried currants

⅓ cup finely chopped maraschino cherries, blotted well on paper towels

about 3 tablespoons coarse decorating sugar

Makes 3 dozen cakes

Raisin-Oat Drops

(from Canada)

These soft, chewy oatmeal cookies come from Nova Scotia—undoubtedly brought there by immigrants from Scotland, where oats claim center stage in many recipes. There are variations that should tickle the fancy of chocolate, coconut or walnut fans. It's hard to miss with this cookie!

1 Preheat oven to 375°F. Grease 3 to 4 large baking sheets. In a medium bowl, combine oats, flour, baking soda, baking powder, ginger, nutmeg, cinnamon and salt; set aside. In a large mixing bowl, beat butter and brown sugar until light and fluffy. Beat in egg, vanilla and orange zest. Stir in maple syrup alternately with flour mixture in 3 additions. Stir in raisins.

2 Drop dough by level tablespoons, 1½ inches apart, on prepared baking sheets. Lightly sprinkle each mound with decorating sugar, being careful not to get sugar on baking sheet.

3 Bake 5 to 8 minutes, or until golden brown around edges. (With accurate oven temperatures, cookies will be soft and chewy at 6 minutes; bake longer for crisp cookies.) Cool on racks. Store in an airtight container at room temperature 1 week; freeze for longer storage.

Variations

Coconut-Oat Drops: Omit raisins; stir 1½ cups flaked or shredded coconut into dough.

Chocolate Chip-Oat Drops: Stir 1 cup semisweet chocolate chips into dough. Omit raisins, if desired.

Nutty Oat Drops: Stir 1 to 1½ cups chopped walnuts or pecans into dough.

1¼ cups rolled oats
1¼ cups all-purpose flour
1 teaspoon baking soda
½ teaspoon baking powder
¾ teaspoon ground ginger
½ teaspoon ground nutmeg
½ teaspoon ground cinnamon
¼ teaspoon salt
½ cup butter, softened
½ cup packed brown sugar
1 egg
2 teaspoons vanilla extract
finely grated zest of 1 medium orange
¾ cup pure maple syrup
1 cup raisins
coarse decorating sugar

Makes about 5 dozen cookies

Sugar Bush Softies

(from the United States)

Soft-cookie lovers will fall head over heels for these tender drops crowned with a shiny maple glaze. The sugaring of the maple trees is an old New England custom still practiced today. Friends bundle against the cold and gather in a "sugar bush"—a grove of sugar maple trees. There they busy themselves collecting the sap, which is then taken to a "sugar house" where it's boiled down. Since it takes about 35 gallons of sap to make one gallon of syrup, their work is cut out for them! Don't confuse real maple syrup with "pancake" syrups, most of which are merely flavored with artificial maple extract . . . and taste like it!

1 Preheat oven to 375°F. Grease 4 large baking sheets. In a medium bowl, combine flour, baking powder, baking soda, nutmeg and salt; set aside. In a large mixing bowl, beat butter until light and fluffy. Beat in maple syrup 2 tablespoons at a time. Add eggs one at a time, beating well after each addition. Stir in flour mixture ½ cup at a time, blending well after each addition. Stir in nuts and raisins. Drop dough by level tablespoons, 1½ inches apart, on prepared baking sheets.

2 Bake cookies 6 to 8 minutes, or just until golden brown around edges. Cool on racks.

3 To prepare Maple Glaze: In a small mixing bowl, combine sugar, milk, vanilla and 2 tablespoons maple syrup. Stir until smooth. Add enough additional maple syrup to make a thick, creamy glaze. Spoon about 1/2 teaspoon glaze onto the top of each cookie; spread with back of spoon. Sprinkle lightly with ground nutmeg. Allow glaze to set before storing cookies in an airtight container at room temperature 1 week; freeze for longer storage.

2 cups all-purpose flour
1 teaspoon baking powder
1 teaspoon baking soda
½ teaspoon ground nutmeg
¼ teaspoon salt
½ cup butter
1 cup pure maple syrup
2 eggs
1 cup chopped walnuts
1 cup raisins
additional ground nutmeg for decoration
Maple Glaze:
2 cups powdered sugar
1 tablespoon milk
2 teaspoons vanilla extract
4 to 6 tablespoons pure maple syrup

Makes about 6½ dozen cookies

Siamese Coconut Milk Cookies

(Tong Ek, *from Thailand*)

These classic Thai cookies are scented with the exotic perfume of coconut milk. Making coconut milk is easy—simply steep unsweetened coconut in hot water and strain! For coconut cream, steep the coconut in hot milk. Dried unsweetened coconut is available at health food stores and the gourmet section of large supermarkets. If you really want to be authentic, use grated fresh coconut!

1 In a medium saucepan, combine coconut and water and bring to boil, stirring occasionally. Remove from heat, cover and let stand 30 minutes. Strain liquid through a sieve into a medium bowl, using the back of a spoon to press out as much liquid as possible. You should have about ½ cup coconut milk. Discard coconut.

2 Preheat oven to 350°F. Grease 3 large baking sheets. In a large bowl, combine flour, baking powder and salt; set aside. In a small mixing bowl, beat butter and brown sugar together until light and fluffy. Beat in egg yolks. Stir in flour mixture alternately with coconut milk in 3 additions, blending well after each. Stir in chopped nuts. Drop dough by heaping teaspoons, 1 inch apart, on prepared baking sheets. Press a whole cashew into center of each mound.

3 Bake 10 to 14 minutes, or until golden brown. Cool on racks. Store cookies in an airtight container at room temperature 1 week; freeze for longer storage.

1 cup dried, unsweetened, flaked coconut

½ cup water

1½ cups all-purpose flour

1 teaspoon baking powder

¼ teaspoon salt

½ cup butter, softened

¾ cup packed brown sugar

2 egg yolks

1 cup finely chopped toasted cashews

about 48 whole toasted cashews

Makes about 4 dozen cookies

Soft Gingerbread Drops

(from the United States)

These old-fashioned favorites are dark, gingery and soft . . . the perfect comfort food for cold winter afternoons. Plan ahead when making them because the dough requires overnight refrigeration for two reasons—so it can become firm enough to work with and to allow the spices to mellow. Chopped dried apricots make a delightful substitute for the raisins.

1 In a medium bowl, combine flour, ginger, cinnamon, nutmeg, baking soda and salt; set aside. In a large mixing bowl, beat shortening, sugar and eggs until well combined. Beat in molasses, vinegar and coffee mixture. Stir in flour mixture ½ cup at a time, blending well after each addition. Stir in raisins and nuts. Cover dough and refrigerate overnight.

2 Preheat oven to 350°F. Grease 4 large baking sheets. Drop dough by heaping tablespoons, 1½ inches apart, on prepared baking sheets. Sprinkle lightly with sugar.

3 Bake 9 to 12 minutes, or until surface springs back when lightly pressed with your fingertip. Cool on racks. Store in an airtight container at room temperature 10 days; freeze for longer storage.

Variation
Double Gingerbread Drops: Stir 1½ to 2 tablespoons finely chopped crystallized ginger into dough with raisins and nuts.

3 cups all-purpose flour
1 tablespoon ground ginger
1 teaspoon ground cinnamon
½ teaspoon ground nutmeg
2 teaspoons baking soda
½ teaspoon salt
½ cup shortening, softened
½ cup granulated sugar
2 eggs
1 cup light unsulphured molasses
1 tablespoon apple cider vinegar or plain vinegar
1 tablespoon instant coffee granules mixed with 1½ teaspoons very hot water
1 cup raisins
1 cup chopped toasted walnuts
coarse decorating sugar or granulated sugar

Makes about 6 dozen cookies

West Indies Banana-Ginger Cookies

Bananas flourish in the West Indies, just as they have since 1516, when Friar Tomás de Berlanga planted the first banana tree on Hispaniola. This pillowy-soft cookie uses banana puree as a flavor base and minced ginger to add pizzazz. Puree the banana easily in a blender or food processor with a metal blade. Lacking that, you can use a fork to mash the banana until no lumps remain. Remember to use very ripe bananas—green fruit just won't give your cookies any flavor.

1 Preheat oven to 375°F. Grease 4 large baking sheets. In a medium bowl, combine flour, baking powder, baking soda, cinnamon, nutmeg, cloves and salt; set aside. In a large mixing bowl, beat butter, sugar and vanilla until light and fluffy. Add eggs 1 at a time, beating well after each addition. Beat in banana puree. Stir in flour mixture ½ cup at a time, blending well after each addition. Stir in ginger and raisins. Drop dough by rounded tablespoons, 1½ inches apart, on prepared baking sheets.

2 Bake 6 to 8 minutes, or until barely golden; cookies should be soft. Dust warm cookies with powdered sugar. Cool on racks. Store in an airtight container at room temperature 1 week; freeze for longer storage.

2 cups all-purpose flour
1 teaspoon baking powder
½ teaspoon baking soda
¾ teaspoon ground cinnamon
½ teaspoon ground nutmeg
¼ teaspoon ground cloves
¼ teaspoon salt
½ cup butter, softened
1 cup granulated sugar
1½ teaspoons vanilla extract
2 eggs
1 cup ripe banana puree (1½ to 2 medium)
⅓ cup minced crystallized ginger
½ cup raisins
powdered sugar

Makes about 5 dozen cookies

HAND-FORMED, PRESSED AND REFRIGERATOR COOKIES

Hand-formed and pressed cookies are the three-dimensional favorites of cookiedom. They're especially popular in Europe, where little girls grow up learning to form and bake these specialties, never knowing there is such a thing as store-bought "slice-and-bake" cookies.

The dough for hand-formed (also called "molded") cookies is generally rich with butter or other fat and, for that reason, is often chilled for easier handling. The process is easy, but takes a little time. Small portions of dough are hand-formed into balls, crescents, braids, logs, rings, pretzels . . . the variety of shapes is endless! Hand-shaped cookie doughs can also be rolled into a log, chilled and sliced, *à la* refrigerator cookies.

Pressed cookies are very professional-looking and much easier than their appearance implies. They're formed using a cookie press or pastry bag fitted with a decorative template or tip. If the dough becomes too soft it will lose its shape when pressed; refrigerate it until it firms slightly. Don't press doughs containing bits of fruit or nuts, which will clog the tips.

Refrigerator cookies are a cook's culinary security. The dough is formed into logs, refrigerated until firm, then cut into slices and baked. Use a knife with a thin, sharp blade to cut the logs, giving them a quarter turn every 6 slices to keep them round. Impatient souls can forego chilling and forming the dough and make drop cookies with it!

Almond Lace Cookies

(Kletskopjes, *from Holland*)

Using brown instead of granulated sugar gives these lacy cookies a rich flavor and beautiful honey-brown hue. During baking, the batter melts to form a cookie so lacy you can see through it. Any nut can be substituted for the almonds; cashews or macadamias make a particularly decadent addition.

1 Preheat oven to 375°F. Grease 3 to 4 large baking sheets. In a large bowl, stir together all ingredients. Form dough into a ball; set aside 5 minutes.

2 Roll level teaspoons of dough into 1-inch balls. Arrange balls, 2 inches apart, on prepared baking sheets and flatten with the bottom of a glass.

3 Bake 5 minutes, or until nicely browned around the edges. Cool on racks. Store in an airtight container at room temperature 5 days; freeze for longer storage. These cookies are very delicate, so store them carefully.

1¼ cups packed brown sugar

¾ cup all-purpose flour

½ teaspoon ground cinnamon

¼ teaspoon ground nutmeg

¼ teaspoon ground allspice

⅛ teaspoon salt

1 cup finely chopped almonds

6 tablespoons butter, softened

Makes about 4 dozen cookies

*Opposite: Orange Butter Cakes (page 130).
Page following: No-Bake Rum-Raisin Balls
(page 128).*

Brandy Ring Twists

(Konjakskränsar, *from Sweden*)

These pretty cookies are formed by twisting two strands of dough together, then forming them into a ring. A cherry slice adds an appealing touch of color. They take a little time, but the beautiful and delicious end results are worth it!

1 In a large mixing bowl, beat butter, sugar and salt together until light and fluffy. Gradually add brandy, then vanilla, beating well to combine. Stir in flour a cup at a time, blending well after each addition. Form dough into a ball; let rest 5 minutes.

2 Preheat oven to 325°F. Lightly grease 3 to 4 large baking sheets. Divide dough in half; refrigerate one half. On a lightly floured surface, roll half of dough out into a 14- x 5-inch rectangle about ¼ inch thick. Use a large knife to cut dough into 56 (5- x ¼-inch) strips.

3 Place two strips of dough side by side and twist together to form a rope. Join ends of rope to form a ring; pinch ends together. Place a maraschino cherry quarter on top of seam; press lightly into dough. Repeat steps 2 and 3 with second half of dough.

4 Arrange rings, 1 inch apart, on prepared baking sheets. Bake 9 to 12 minutes, or until barely golden.

5 While cookies are baking, prepare glaze. Combine glaze ingredients in a small saucepan and cook over medium heat, stirring constantly, *just* until sugar dissolves. Brush hot glaze over hot cookies while still on baking sheets.

1 cup butter, softened
¾ cup granulated sugar
¼ teaspoon salt
¼ cup brandy
1 teaspoon vanilla extract
2½ cups all-purpose flour
13-14 maraschino cherries, blotted well on paper towels and cut into quarters
Brandy Glaze
½ cup powdered sugar
¼ cup brandy

Makes about 4½ dozen cookies

Opposite: Raisin Rusks (page 139).
Page preceding: Pigtails (page 135).

Cats' Tongues

(Lenguas de Gato, *from Spain*)

Found in pastry shops all over Madrid, these delicate, ultra-thin wafers are wonderful partners for ice cream, puddings or custards. They're tender, light and crispy . . . simple, yet provocative. Can you tell I love them? This cookie is made with a different technique than most: The batter is spooned into a pastry bag and piped onto the baking sheets. If you don't have a pastry bag, it's easy to make one out of waxed paper; see page 148.

1 Preheat oven to 425°F. Grease and flour 3 to 4 large baking sheets; set aside. In a small mixing bowl, beat butter, sugar and salt until light and fluffy. Add vanilla and egg whites, one at a time, beating well after each addition, then continue to beat 2 minutes at a medium speed. Stir in flour 2 tablespoons at a time, blending well after each addition.

2 Spoon mixture into a pastry bag fitted with a plain ¼-inch round tip (#11 or #12). Pipe onto prepared baking sheets in 3-inch-long "pencils," about 2 inches apart.

3 Bake 5 to 7 minutes, or until edges of cookies are golden brown; centers will remain pale. Cool on racks. Store in an airtight container at room temperature 4 to 5 days; freeze for longer storage.

Variations
Nutty Cats' Tongues: Stir ⅓ cup very finely chopped toasted almonds, hazelnuts or walnuts into batter.

⅓ cup butter, softened

⅔ cup granulated sugar

pinch of salt

½ teaspoon vanilla extract

3 egg whites

½ cup all-purpose flour

Makes about 5 dozen cookies

Chocolate-Filled Cats' Tongues: In the top of a double boiler, combine 3 ounces semisweet chocolate and 3 tablespoons butter. Stir
over simmering water until melted and smooth. Pour into small
mixing bowl and beat at medium speed 1 minute. Stir in ¾ cup
powdered sugar; beat until thick enough to spread. Spread the
bottoms of half the cookies with chocolate filling; top with second
cookie to form a sandwich.

Jam-Filled Cats' Tongues: Spread a thin layer of orange marmalade
or seedless red raspberry preserves on the bottoms of half the
cookies; top with second cookie to form a sandwich. If desired, dip
1 inch of both ends of cookie sandwich into melted semisweet
chocolate (about 4 ounces).

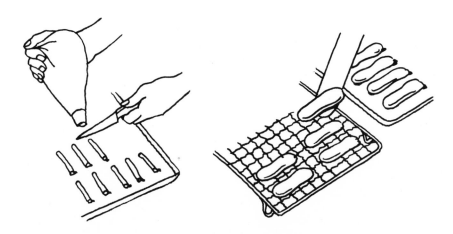

Chinese Almond Cookies

(Hsing-jen-ping)

When I was growing up in Denver, our family made a monthly visit to The Lotus Room—a Chinese restaurant noted for its exquisite egg rolls. But I thought the almond cookies were the best thing on the menu. That delicious childhood memory is happily relived in these incredibly rich and crumbly cookies. Lard is the magic ingredient that makes them so meltingly crisp. You can substitute shortening or butter . . . but you won't get a cookie that makes memories!

1 In a medium bowl, combine flour, baking powder, baking soda and salt; set aside. In a large mixing bowl, beat lard, sugars and almond extract until light and fluffy. Beat in egg. Stir in flour mixture ½ cup at a time, blending well after each addition; dough will be very soft. Spoon into the center of a 15-inch length of plastic wrap. Fold long sides of plastic over dough. With your palms, roll wrapped dough into a log 12 inches long and about 2 inches in diameter. Twist ends of plastic wrap to seal. Freeze or refrigerate until firm, 1 to 4 hours.

2 Preheat oven to 350°F. Grease 3 to 4 large baking sheets. Cut chilled dough into ¼-inch-thick slices. Arrange, 1½ inches apart, on prepared baking sheets. Lightly press a whole almond into the center of each cookie. Brush rounds with egg glaze.

3 Bake 11 to 14 minutes, or until golden brown. Cool on racks. Store in an airtight container at room temperature 1 week; freeze for longer storage.

2½ cups all-purpose flour
1 teaspoon baking powder
½ teaspoon baking soda
¼ teaspoon salt
1 cup lard, softened
½ cup granulated sugar
½ cup packed brown sugar
2 teaspoons almond extract
1 egg
about 48 whole blanched almonds
1 egg yolk beaten with 2 teaspoons water for glaze

Makes about 4 dozen cookies

Calcutta Coconut Cookies

(Nan Khatai, *from India*)

I find this light, crisp cookie particularly appealing with tart sherbets or ices. The recipe calls for commercial sweetened coconut because it's readily available; my personal preference, however, is to coat the cookies with dried unsweetened coconut. The result is a cookie with less sweetness and more natural coconut flavor. You can find unsweetened coconut in health food stores and the gourmet section of large supermarkets.

1 Preheat oven to 375°F. Grease and flour 4 large baking sheets. In a medium bowl, combine flour, baking powder, baking soda, cardamom and salt; set aside. In a large mixing bowl, beat butter and sugar together until light and fluffy. Beat in egg. Stir in flour mixture ½ cup at a time, blending well after each addition.

2 Place coconut in a shallow medium bowl. Form rounded teaspoons of dough into 1-inch balls; roll each ball in coconut. Arrange, 1½ inches apart, on prepared baking sheets. Use the bottom of a glass to flatten mounds to about ¼-inch thickness; if necessary, dip bottom of glass into flour occasionally to prevent sticking.

3 Bake cookies 10 to 14 minutes, or until golden brown. Cool on racks. Store in an airtight container at room temperature 1 week; freeze for longer storage.

2 cups all-purpose flour
1 teaspoon baking powder
½ teaspoon baking soda
1 teaspoon ground cardamom
¼ teaspoon salt
¾ cup + 2 tablespoons butter, softened
1 cup granulated sugar
1 egg
about 1½ cups flaked or shredded coconut

Makes about 5 dozen cookies

Crisp Vanilla-Sugar Cookies

(from the United States)

This old-fashioned recipe produces big cookies that are thin and buttery-crisp. A vanilla-sugar topping adds a fragrant finish to a cookie that's good enough for special company.

1 In a large mixing bowl, beat butter, sugar, salt and vanilla together until light and fluffy. Add sour cream and flour alternately in 3 additions, blending well after each. Spoon dough onto the center of a 12-inch length of plastic wrap. Fold long sides of plastic wrap over dough. With palms, roll wrapped dough into a log 2½ inches in diameter. Twist ends of plastic to seal. Freeze or refrigerate until firm, 1 to 4 hours.

2 Preheat oven to 350°F. Grease 4 large baking sheets. Have some cool water handy in a small bowl; set aside. Remove dough from refrigerator and unwrap. Cut chilled dough into ⅛-inch-thick slices. Arrange, 2 inches apart, on prepared baking sheets. Brush lightly with water. Sprinkle liberally with vanilla sugar, being careful not to get any on baking sheet.

3 Bake 11 to 15 minutes, or until edges are golden brown. Let stand on baking sheets 30 seconds before carefully removing to racks. Cookies will be fragile. Store in an airtight container at room temperature 10 days; freeze for longer storage.

---

1 cup butter, softened

1½ cups granulated sugar

¼ teaspoon salt

2 teaspoons vanilla extract

½ cup sour cream

2 cups all-purpose flour

about ½ cup Vanilla Sugar, page 16

Makes about 4½ dozen cookies

Variations

Brown Sugar Cookies: Substitute 1½ cups packed brown sugar for the granulated sugar; sprinkle tops of cookies with sieved brown sugar instead of vanilla sugar.

Chocolate Sugar Cookies: Increase granulated sugar to 2 cups, decrease flour to 1¾ cups and add ½ cup unsweetened cocoa power. Combine cocoa with flour before adding to butter mixture. Sprinkle tops of cookies with coarse decorating or regular granulated sugar instead of vanilla sugar.

Spiced Sugar Cookies: Add ½ teaspoon ground cinnamon and ¼ teaspoon *each* ground ginger, allspice and cloves to flour before adding to butter mixture.

Colombian Coffee Cookies

Colombia is one of the world's major coffee producers, so it's only natural that Colombian cooks use this favorite beverage not only for drinking but for cooking as well. I use instant coffee powder in this cookie because it delivers more potent flavor than brewed coffee would supply. Dark rum adds its subtle nuance and toasted cashews lend crunch.

1 Preheat oven to 375°F. Grease 3 or 4 large baking sheets. To prepare cookies: In a medium bowl, combine flour, baking powder and salt; set aside. In a large mixing bowl, beat butter, sugar and coffee powder until light and fluffy. Add rum a tablespoon at a time, beating well after each addition. Stir in flour mixture ½ cup at a time, blending well after each addition. Stir in chopped nuts.

2 With floured hands, roll heaping tablespoons of dough into balls. Arrange, 1½ inches apart, on prepared baking sheets. Use the bottom of a glass or a decorative cookie stamp to flatten balls to ½-inch thickness.

3 Bake 10 to 15 minutes, or until golden on the bottom. To prepare Coffee Glaze: While cookies are baking, in a small bowl, combine sugar, coffee powder and rum. Add enough milk to make a thin, creamy glaze. Brush glaze over warm cookies while still on baking sheets. Lightly press a coffee bean candy or cashew into top of each cookie. Cool on racks. Store cookies in an airtight container at room temperature 1 week; freeze for longer storage.

Cookies

3 cups all-purpose flour
2 teaspoons baking powder
½ teaspoon salt
¾ cup butter, softened
1 cup granulated sugar
2 tablespoons instant coffee powder (not granules)
⅓ cup dark rum
1 cup chopped toasted cashew nuts
48 coffee-bean-shaped candies or unsalted toasted cashew halves, or salted cashew halves that have been rinsed and dried on paper towels

Coffee Glaze

½ cup powdered sugar
½ teaspoon instant coffee powder
1½ teaspoons dark rum
1½ teaspoons to 1½ tablespoons milk

Makes about 4 dozen cookies

Danish Dandies

(Danske Småkager)

I imagine these delightful cookies got their name from their wonderful light lemon flavor . . . it certainly is dandy! Sieved hard-cooked eggs add richness and give these tiny cookies a lovely soft texture; you'll have an easier time of it if you cut the eggs into quarters before sieving. The dough must be refrigerated overnight to facilitate handling, so plan ahead. In a pinch, freeze the dough for three hours instead.

1 In a large mixing bowl, beat butter, sugar and salt together until light and fluffy. Add sieved eggs, lemon zest and vanilla and blend well. Add flour ¾ cup at a time, stirring well after each addition. Form dough into a ball and wrap in plastic. Refrigerate overnight or place in freezer 3 hours.

2 Preheat oven to 350°F. Lightly grease 3 to 4 large baking sheets. With floured hands, roll scant teaspoons of dough into 1-inch balls. Arrange, 1 inch apart, on prepared baking sheets. Press an almond into the center of each; balls will become slightly oval in shape.

3 In a small saucepan, heat corn syrup just until it thins slightly. Brush warm syrup over cookies.

4 Bake 8 to 11 minutes, or until barely golden. Cool on racks. Store in an airtight container at room temperature 5 days; freeze for longer storage.

1 cup butter, softened
¾ cup granulated sugar
½ teaspoon salt
3 hard-cooked eggs, sieved
finely grated zest of 1 large lemon
1½ teaspoons vanilla extract
2 cups all-purpose flour
about 72 whole blanched almonds
about ¼ cup light corn syrup

Makes about 6 dozen cookies

Ribbon Cookies

(**Hindbaerkager,** *from Denmark)*

Scandinavian cooks are noted for their baking skills and these beautiful but easy cookies are a perfect example. Long strips of rich sugar-cookie dough are ribboned with sparkling red raspberry jam. The cookie strips are then cut on the diagonal to create small, colorful bites of pure pleasure.

1 Preheat oven to 375°F. Grease 2 large baking sheets. In a large mixing bowl, beat butter, sugar and salt together until light and fluffy. Add egg and vanilla; beat to combine. Stir in flour ½ cup at a time, blending well after each addition. Form dough into a ball; let rest 5 minutes.

2 Divide dough into sixths; place on a lightly floured work surface. Using your palms, roll each portion back and forth on the work surface into a rope ¾ inch in diameter. Place 3 ropes, 2 inches apart, on each prepared baking sheet. With the side of your little finger, press a groove (to within ¼ inch of baking sheet) down the center of each rope.

3 Bake 10 minutes. Remove baking sheets from oven. Spoon jam into cookie grooves. Return to oven; bake an additional 6 to 10 minutes, or until pale golden brown.

4 While cookies are baking, prepare glaze: In a small bowl, combine sugar, vanilla and 1 tablespoon milk. Add enough additional milk to make a smooth and creamy glaze of medium consistency.

5 Remove cookies from oven; cool on baking sheets 5 minutes. Drizzle warm cookies with glaze; let stand 3 minutes. Cut cookie strips at a 45-degree angle into 1-inch slices. Transfer to racks to cool. Store in an airtight container at room temperature 5 days.

1 cup butter, softened

⅔ cup granulated sugar

¼ teaspoon salt

1 egg

1 teaspoon vanilla extract

2⅔ cups all-purpose flour

about ½ cup seedless red raspberry jam

Glaze

½ cup powdered sugar

¾ teaspoon vanilla extract

1 to 2 tablespoons milk

Makes about 5 dozen cookies

French Butter Cakes

(Madeleines, *from France*)

In his landmark novel Remembrance of Things Past, *French novelist Marcel Proust immortalized the* madeleine *when he wrote, "I raised to my lips a spoonful of the cake . . . a shudder ran through my whole body and I stopped, intent upon the extraordinary changes that were taking place." Proust's passion for this classic sponge-cake cookie has been shared with countless others for centuries. It requires special shell-shaped molds, which can easily be found in kitchen equipment shops.*

1 Preheat oven to 375°F. Butter and flour 12 (3-inch) madeleine molds; set aside. In a small mixing bowl, beat eggs, vanilla and salt at high speed until light. Beating constantly, gradually add sugar; continue beating at high speed until mixture is thick and pale and ribbons form in bowl when beaters are lifted, 5 to 10 minutes. Sift flour into egg mixture 1/3 at a time, gently folding after each addition. Add lemon zest, then pour melted butter around edge of batter. Quickly but gently fold butter into batter. Spoon batter into prepared molds; it will mound slightly above tops.

2 Bake 14 to 17 minutes, or until cakes are golden and the tops spring back when gently pressed with your fingertip. Use the tip of a knife to loosen madeleines from pan; invert onto rack. Immediately sprinkle warm cookies with granulated sugar. Madeleines are best eaten the day they're baked. Leftover madeleines are wonderful when dunked into coffee or tea.

Variation
Chocolate Madeleines: Omit lemon zest. Increase sugar to 1/2 cup. Substitute 1/4 cup unsweetened cocoa powder for 2 tablespoons of the flour; sift into batter with flour.

2 eggs

3/4 teaspoon vanilla extract

1/8 teaspoon salt

1/3 cup granulated sugar

1/2 cup all-purpose flour

finely grated zest of 1 small lemon

1/4 cup butter, melted and cooled to
    room temperature

additional granulated sugar for
    topping

***Makes about 1 dozen 3-inch
cookies***

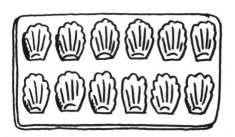

Orange Custard Cookies

(Mirlitons, *from France*)

These tiny, two-bite cookies consist of flaky pastry cup with an almond-custard filling. As it bakes, the filling forms a sparkling crust, giving these delicate treasures a beautiful finish. Mixing the custard in a 2-cup glass measure makes it easy to pour into the cookie-dough cups. This recipe calls for orange flower water, which is a distillation or orange blossoms and has the fragrance of summer sunshine.

1 To prepare crust: In a medium bowl, combine flour, sugar and salt. Use a pastry blender or 2 knives to cut in butter until mixture resembles coarse crumbs, or process in a food processor using pulses. Stir in egg. If necessary, stir in ice water, a few drops at a time, just until dough holds together. Knead dough 15 seconds; form into a ball. Cover and set aside 15 minutes.

2 To prepare filling: In a medium bowl, blend all filling ingredients. Set aside.

3 Preheat oven to 350°F. Lightly grease 24 miniature (1¾- x ¾-inch) muffin tins. On a lightly floured surface, roll dough out into a rough circle ⅛ inch thick. Cut out dough using a floured 2½-inch scalloped cutter. Gather and reroll dough scraps. Place one round in each prepared muffin tin, pressing firmly over bottom and sides. Fill each shell about half full with custard mixture.

4 Bake about 25 minutes, or until crust is golden brown and a knife inserted into center of custard comes out clean. Use the tip of a pointed knife to loosen and remove cookies from tins; cool on racks. Store in an airtight container in refrigerator 5 days. Do not freeze.

Cookie Crust

2 cups all-purpose flour
3 tablespoons granulated sugar
⅛ teaspoon salt
¾ cup cold butter, cut into 12 pieces
1 egg, lightly beaten
about 1 tablespoon ice water

Custard

2 eggs, lightly beaten
⅔ cup whipping cream
⅔ cup granulated sugar
¾ cup finely ground almonds
finely grated zest of ½ small orange
2 teaspoons orange flower water, or 1 teaspoon vanilla extract
⅛ teaspoon ground nutmeg
⅛ teaspoon salt

Makes 2 dozen cookies

Georgetown Lime Cookies

(Broas, *from British Guyana)*

Both fresh lime juice and lime zest add citrus sparkle to these tart, refreshing cookies. You can substitute lemon juice and zest for an equally lively taste. When grating any citrus fruit, be sure to take only the colored portion of the rind; the white part is bitter. For a nice variation, add either 1 cup toasted almonds or grated coconut to the dough just before you roll it into balls.

1 Preheat oven to 350°F. Grease 3 to 4 large baking sheets. In a medium bowl, combine flour, baking powder, salt, nutmeg and cinnamon; set aside. In a large mixing bowl, beat butter, sugar and lime zest until light and fluffy. Gradually beat in lime juice. Stir in flour mixture ½ cup at a time, blending well after each addition.

2 Place sugar-spice mixture in a small bowl. Roll rounded teaspoons of dough into 1-inch balls. Roll balls in sugar-spice mixture; arrange, 1 inch apart, on prepared baking sheets. Use a decorative cookie stamp or the bottom of a glass to flatten balls slightly.

3 Bake 13 to 16 minutes, or until deep golden brown on the bottom. Cool on racks. Store in an airtight container at room temperature 1 week; freeze for longer storage.

2 cups all-purpose flour
1 teaspoon baking powder
¼ teaspoon salt
¼ teaspoon ground nutmeg
¼ teaspoon ground cinnamon
¾ cup butter, softened
1 cup granulated sugar
finely grated zest of 2 limes
3 tablespoons fresh lime juice
⅓ cup granulated sugar mixed with ¼ teaspoon each ground nutmeg and cinnamon for topping

Makes about 5 dozen cookies

Greek Honey Cookies

(Melomakarona)

It's said that Venetian bakers brought this orange-scented cookie to Greece in the 15th century when certain Greek islands were under Italian rule. Traditionally, the cookies are dipped in a honey syrup . . . and I've given you that rendition. Personally, however, I love them crisp, without the honey dip.

1 Preheat oven to 325°F. In a medium bowl, combine flour, baking powder, baking soda, cinnamon, cloves and salt; set aside. In a large mixing bowl, beat butter and sugar until light and fluffy. Gradually drizzle in cognac and orange juice, beating at medium speed until combined. Stir in orange zest, then flour mixture ½ cup at a time, blending well after each addition.

2 With floured hands, roll heaping tablespoons of dough into egg shapes about 1½ inches long. Arrange, 1½ inches apart, on 3 to 4 large *ungreased* baking sheets. Use a decorative cookie stamp or other utensil to imprint and flatten cookies to ¼- to ⅜-inch thick.

3 Bake 15 to 20 minutes, or until golden brown. Cool on racks.

4 To prepare honey syrup: In a medium saucepan over medium-high heat, combine all ingredients. Bring to a boil. Reduce heat to low and simmer, uncovered, 5 minutes. Remove from heat.

5 Line 2 baking sheets with waxed paper. Set racks over baking sheets. Add a few cookies at a time to warm syrup; turn to coat all sides. Using a slotted spoon, transfer cookies to racks. *Lightly* sprinkle each cookie with pistachios, allowing the design to show through the nuts. Set aside overnight to dry. Store in an airtight container at room temperature 1 week; freeze for longer storage.

3 cups all-purpose flour
1½ teaspoons baking powder
½ teaspoon baking soda
¾ teaspoon ground cinnamon
½ teaspoon ground cloves
½ teaspoon salt
1¼ cups butter, softened
¾ cup granulated sugar
3 tablespoons cognac or brandy
3 tablespoons orange juice
finely grated zest of ½ medium orange
about ½ cup coarsely ground toasted pistachio nuts

Honey Syrup

1¼ cups honey
¾ cup sugar
1 cup water
½ teaspoon ground cinnamon

Makes about 4½ dozen cookies

Hussars' Kisses

(Huszarcsok, from Hungary)

It's said that these cookies were named after the Hungarian light cavalry of the 15th century. According to legend, the kisses of those daring soldiers were deliciously sweet and, because the soldiers were always on the move, disappeared quickly. These namesake cookies live up to that legend with their rich hazelnut flavor accented with a deliciously sweet crown of raspberry jam. Needless to say, they also disappear very quickly.

1 In a medium bowl, combine flour, ground nuts, baking powder and salt; set aside. In a large mixing bowl, cream butter and sugar until light and fluffy. Beat in egg and vanilla. Stir in flour mixture ½ cup at a time, blending well after each addition. Cover and refrigerate 30 minutes.

2 Preheat oven to 375°F. Grease 2 to 3 large baking sheets. Place chopped nuts in a medium bowl. With lightly floured hands, roll teaspoons of dough into 1-inch balls. Roll balls in chopped nuts. Arrange, 1 inch apart, on prepared baking sheets. Using your little finger, make an indentation about ½ inch deep in the center of each ball. Fill depressions with jam or a cherry half.

3 Bake cookies 10 to 14 minutes, or until golden brown. Cool on racks. Store in an airtight container at room temperature 5 days; freeze for longer storage.

Variation

Chocolate Hussars' Kisses: Substitute ⅓ cup unsweetened cocoa powder for ¼ cup flour; increase sugar to 1 cup.

1½ cups all-purpose flour
¾ cup ground hazelnuts
1 teaspoon baking powder
⅛ teaspoon salt
¾ cup butter, softened
¾ cup granulated sugar
1 egg
1 teaspoon vanilla extract
1½ cups finely chopped hazelnuts
about ½ cup seedless raspberry jam or jelly, or about 40 maraschino cherry halves

Makes about 3½ dozen cookies

Italian Anise Cookies

(Biscotti d'Anici)

A Venetian creation loved by both Northern and Southern Italians is the versatile biscotto. *This popular favorite comes in many variations, but this version is my favorite. Italians love to dunk the intensely crunchy* biscotti *in dessert wine or espresso.*

1 Preheat oven to 325°F. Generously grease 2 large baking sheets. In a large mixing bowl, beat butter, sugar, salt, orange zest, lemon zest and anise seed until light. Add eggs one at a time, beating well after each addition. Stir in flour, baking powder, baking soda and nuts.

2 Divide dough into thirds. With buttered fingers, shape each portion of dough into a log about 12 inches long and 1½ inches in diameter. Place 2 logs, 4 inches apart, on one baking sheet, the third log on the other baking sheet. Using your palms, flatten logs slightly to about 1-inch thickness. Bake 25 minutes, rotating baking sheets top to bottom midway through baking.

3 Remove cookies from oven; reduce heat to 275°F. Using a thin-bladed knife, cut rolls at a 45-degree angle into ¾-inch slices. Lay slices, cut side down, 1½ inches apart on baking sheets. Bake an additional 40 minutes, or until very dry.

4 Cool cookies on racks. Store in an airtight container at room temperature 10 days; freeze for longer storage.

Variation

Chocolate-Dipped Biscotti: Melt 6 ounces semisweet chocolate; place in a small bowl. Line 2 large baking sheets with waxed paper. Dip ¾ inch of both ends of cooled cookies into melted chocolate.

½ cup butter, softened
1⅓ cups granulated sugar
½ teaspoon salt
finely grated zest of 1 medium orange
finely grated zest of 1 medium lemon
1 tablespoon anise seed
3 eggs
3 cups all-purpose flour
2½ teaspoons baking powder
½ teaspoon baking soda
2 cups sliced toasted almonds, coarsely chopped

Makes about 4 dozen cookies

Opposite: Sesame-Anise Melts (page 142). Page following: Kay's "Sneak"erdoodles (page 143).

Kahlúa-Pecan Pie Cookies

(from the United States)

My mother, who grew up in the South, gave me the recipe for these unique and irresistible cookies—but I confess that the touch of Kahlúa is mine. The filling and cookie dough must be made in advance and refrigerated so they're easier to work with. If need be, both may be refrigerated for up to 5 days.

1 To prepare dough: In a large mixing bowl, beat butter, brown sugar and salt until light and fluffy. Beat in egg, corn syrup and Kahlúa. Stir in flour ½ cup at a time, blending well after each addition. Cover and refrigerate 4 hours.

2 To prepare filling: In a small saucepan, combine butter, corn syrup and sugar. Cook over medium heat, stirring occasionally, *just* until mixture comes to a full boil. Immediately remove from heat; stir in pecans and Kahlúa. Refrigerate 1 hour or until firm. Roll half-teaspoons of mixture into balls (you should have about 72). Place balls on a plate; cover and freeze until ready to use.

3 Preheat oven to 375°F. Grease 4 large baking sheets. Roll heaping teaspoons of dough into balls and arrange, 1½ inches apart, on prepared baking sheets. Use the tip of a wooden spoon handle to make a ½-inch-deep indentation in the center of each ball; dip handle tip in cold water between uses.

4 Bake 5 minutes. Remove from oven. Firmly press a ball of filling into the center of each cookie. Return to oven; continue to bake 5 minutes or until golden brown on the bottom.

Opposite: Chocolate-Mint Cookie Sandwiches (page 156).
Page preceding: Double Fudge Brownies (page 164).

Cookie Dough

1 cup butter, softened
⅔ cup packed brown sugar
¼ teaspoon salt
1 egg
⅓ cup dark corn syrup
2½ tablespoons Kahlúa or other coffee liqueur
2½ cups all-purpose flour

Pecan Filling

¼ cup butter
¼ cup dark corn syrup
⅔ cup powdered sugar
¾ cup finely chopped toasted pecans
1 tablespoon Kahlúa or other coffee liqueur

Makes about 6 dozen cookies

Macaroon Jam Slices

(Makronen-Schnitten, *from Austria*)

With just four basic ingredients, these cookies are among the quickest and easiest to make. An almond macaroon mixture is formed into a long log (later cut into slices) with a center groove, which holds a delicious cargo of jam. Apricot is traditional, but a dark-colored jam (such as blackberry or red raspberry) makes a more striking contrast.

1 Preheat oven to 350°F. Grease 2 large baking sheets. In a large bowl, combine all ingredients except jam; mixture should form a paste.

2 Sprinkle a work surface lightly with powdered sugar. Divide dough into four parts. Using your palms, roll each part back and forth on work surface into a rope ¾ inch in diameter and about 11 inches long. Place 2 ropes, 3 inches apart, on each prepared baking sheet. With the side of your little finger, press a groove (to within ¼ inch of baking sheet) down the center of each rope, leaving ¼ inch at each end of rolls.

3 Bake 10 minutes. Remove from oven; spoon jam into grooves. Return to oven and bake 10 to 15 more minutes, or until golden brown. Cool on racks. Cut cookie strips at a 45-degree angle into 1-inch slices. Store in an airtight container at room temperature 1 week; freeze for longer storage.

2 cups finely ground almonds

⅓ cup granulated sugar

1 egg white

¼ teaspoon almond extract

⅛ teaspoon salt

about ½ cup apricot or other jam, stirred until smooth

powdered sugar

Makes about 3½ dozen cookies

Melting Moments

(from Scotland)

Scotland's climate isn't favorable for growing wheat, so oats have been a staple since ancient times. Here they're used subtly: The dough is rolled in oats just before baking to give the cookies a light, crunchy cloak of toasty oat flavor. These cookies are aptly named because of their dreamy melt-in-your-mouth texture. You don't have to be Scottish to love them!

1 Preheat oven to 375°F. Grease 3 to 4 large baking sheets. In a medium bowl, combine flour, cornstarch and salt; set aside. In a large mixing bowl, beat butter, lard and sugar together until light and fluffy. Beat in egg and vanilla. Stir in flour mixture ½ cup at a time, blending well after each addition.

2 Place oats in a small bowl. Lightly dampen hands with water. Roll heaping teaspoons of dough into 1-inch balls; roll balls in oats, re-dampening hands as necessary. Arrange balls, 1½ inches apart, on prepared baking sheets.

3 Bake 11 to 14 minutes, or until golden on the tops and golden brown on the bottoms. Cool on racks. Store cookies in an airtight container at room temperature 1 week; freeze for longer storage.

1½ cups all-purpose flour
¾ cup cornstarch
½ teaspoon salt
⅔ cup butter, softened
⅓ cup lard or shortening, softened
¾ cup granulated sugar
1 egg
2 teaspoons vanilla extract
about 1½ cups quick-cooking rolled oats

Makes about 5 dozen cookies

No-Bake Rum-Raisin Balls

(from New Zealand)

My friend Rhoda Harwood brought me this recipe from Christchurch, New Zealand. Unlike American rum or bourbon balls, these are freighted with raisins and coconut, and don't use ground cookie crumbs as a base. Orange juice can be substituted, but the flavor of the rum is surprisingly subtle. Rum-Raisin Balls must be made a day in advance to let the flavors mellow and to allow the cookies to firm.

1 In a large bowl, combine rum and oats; cover and set aside 1 hour. Add all remaining ingredients *except* granulated sugar; stir until well combined. Cover and refrigerate 1 hour.

2 Roll teaspoons of mixture into 1-inch balls. Place sugar in a small bowl. Roll balls in sugar, coating each generously.

3 Store 24 hours in an airtight container at room temperature before serving. May be stored, airtight, 10 days; freeze for longer storage.

⅓ cup dark rum

⅓ cup rolled oats

2 cups powdered sugar

3 tablespoons unsweetened cocoa powder

⅔ cup chopped toasted walnuts

⅔ cup golden raisins

⅔ cup shredded coconut

¼ teaspoon ground nutmeg

¼ teaspoon ground cinnamon

⅓ cup butter, melted and cooled

about 3 tablespoons granulated sugar

Makes about 3 dozen cookies

Nut-Filled Cigar Cookies

(Jevisli, from Armenia)

These cigar-shaped cookies are perfumed with orange flower water, a popular Middle Eastern flavoring. The dough is soft and must be shaped by hand. If you find it sticking to your fingers, simply dust your hands lightly with flour. These cookies don't keep well, so any you won't eat within a couple of days should be frozen for future enjoyment.

1 To prepare cookie dough: In a large mixing bowl, beat butter, sugar, orange flower water and salt until light and fluffy. Beat in egg. Stir in flour, ½ cup at a time, blending well after each addition. Form dough into a ball; cover and refrigerate 20 minutes.

2 To prepare filling: In a medium bowl, combine nuts, sugar and cinnamon. Add butter and stir to combine.

3 Preheat oven to 350°F. Grease 2 large baking sheets. Roll heaping tablespoons of dough into 2-inch ovals. Use the side of your little finger to press an indentation lengthwise down the center of each oval. Spoon about ½ teaspoon filling into indentation. Bring sides of dough up over filling and pinch to seal. Roll oval between your palms to form a 3½-inch cigar shape. Arrange cookies, seam side down and 1 inch apart, on prepared baking sheets. Use a sharp knife to cut 3 crosswise slashes, ½ inch apart, in the top of each cookie. Brush cookies with egg glaze.

4 Bake 17 to 22 minutes, or until golden on top and golden brown on the bottom. Cool on racks. Store in an airtight container at room temperature 3 days; freeze for longer storage.

Cookie Dough

1 cup butter, softened
¾ cup granulated sugar
2 teaspoons orange flower water
¼ teaspoon salt
1 egg
2½ cups all-purpose flour
1 egg white beaten with 2 teaspoons water for glaze

Nut Filling

⅓ cup finely chopped toasted walnuts
⅓ cup granulated sugar
½ teaspoon ground cinnamon
1 tablespoon butter, melted

Makes about 3 dozen cookies

129

Orange Butter Cakes

(Biscotins, *from France*)

These tiny, Grand Marnier-scented cakes hail from France's Languedoc region. A Grand Marnier-kissed glaze adds a sophisticated finishing touch to these crisp cookies.

1 Preheat oven to 350°F. *Generously* grease about 18 (2½-inch) tartlet or cupcake tins. In a medium bowl, combine flour, baking powder and salt; set aside. In a large bowl, beat butter and sugar together until light and fluffy. Blend in vanilla and egg, then add Grand Marnier 1 tablespoon at a time, beating well after each addition. Stir in flour mixture ½ cup at a time, blending well after each addition. Stir in orange peel.

2 Fill prepared tins about ⅔ full. Use your fingertips to press dough into tins so it conforms to sides; even top of dough. Arrange tartlet tins on a large baking sheet. Bake 15 to 18 minutes, or until golden brown. Let cakes rest in tins 3 minutes. Turn out of molds onto a rack over waxed paper. If necessary, use the tip of a knife to loosen cakes from molds. Leave cakes upside down; the bottoms will become the tops of these cookies.

3 While cookies are baking, prepare glaze. In a medium bowl, combine sugar and 4 tablespoons Grand Marnier. Add enough additional Grand Marnier to make a smooth, creamy glaze of medium consistency. Spoon over warm cookies, covering tops and allowing glaze to drizzle down sides. If desired, lightly sprinkle glazed cookies with minced candied orange peel. Cool completely on racks. Store in an airtight container at room temperature 3 to 4 days; freeze for longer storage.

1¾ cups all-purpose flour
1 teaspoon baking powder
⅛ teaspoon salt
½ cup butter, softened
⅔ cup granulated sugar
1 teaspoon vanilla extract
1 egg
¼ cup Grand Marnier
½ cup finely chopped candied orange peel
Grand Marnier Glaze
1½ cups powdered sugar
4 to 6 tablespoons Grand Marnier or other orange liqueur
about 3 tablespoons minced candied orange peel, optional

Makes about 1½ dozen cookies

Orange Flower–Almond Cookies

(El Menenas, *from Egypt*)

This pretty cookie has a dome of almond paste that has been scented with orange flower water. Orange flower water is a distillation of bitter-orange blossoms; it can be found in liquor stores and Middle Eastern markets.

1 Preheat oven to 350°F. Grease 2 large baking sheets. In a medium bowl, combine flour, baking powder and cinnamon; set aside. In a large mixing bowl, beat butter, sugar and orange flower water until light and fluffy. Stir in flour mixture, ½ cup at a time, blending well after each addition. Form dough into a ball. Wrap in waxed paper or plastic wrap; refrigerate 20 minutes.

2 In a small mixing bowl, beat almond paste, butter, sugar, cinnamon and orange flower water together until smooth. Roll ½ teaspoons of almond paste mixture into smooth balls; set aside.

3 Roll heaping tablespoons of dough into 1½-inch balls. Arrange, 1 inch apart, on prepared baking sheets. Use your thumb to make a ½-inch-deep indentation in each ball; fill indentation with an almond paste ball.

4 Bake 15 to 18 minutes, or until bottoms of cookies are golden brown and dome of almond paste is lightly browned. If desired, sprinkle hot cookies with granulated sugar. Cool on racks. Store in an airtight container at room temperature 1 week; freeze for longer storage.

Cookie

2 cups all-purpose flour
½ teaspoon baking powder
¼ teaspoon ground cinnamon
¾ cup butter, softened
½ cup granulated sugar
1¾ teaspoons orange flower water

Almond Paste Filling

3 ounces almond paste, softened
1 tablespoon butter, softened
⅓ cup granulated sugar
¼ teaspoon ground cinnamon
½ teaspoon orange flower water
additional granulated sugar (optional)

Makes about 1½ dozen cookies

Peanut Butter 'n Jellies

(from the United States)

My husband Ron, a true peanut-butter-cookie monster, gives these a triple blue ribbon—with or without the jelly! To this day, whenever we visit his 90-year-old grandmother Flossie, there's a huge batch of these favorites waiting for him. Flossie declares that beating the moist ingredients for at least 5 minutes is what makes her cookies so crisp and light . . . I agree! Shortening also contributes to this cookies' lightness.

1 Preheat oven to 350°F. Grease 4 large baking sheets. In a medium bowl, combine flour, baking soda and salt; set aside. In a large mixing bowl, beat shortening, peanut butter, sugars and vanilla together until light and fluffy. Add eggs one at a time, beating well after each addition. Beat at medium speed 5 minutes, scraping bowl as necessary. Stir in flour mixture ½ cup at a time, blending well after each addition.

2 Roll rounded tablespoons of dough into balls. Arrange, 1½ inches apart, on prepared baking sheets. With the bottom of a glass, flatten balls to about ⅜-inch thickness. Use your thumb to make an indentation, almost to the baking sheet, in the center of each cookie.

3 Bake 10 to 13 minutes, or until golden brown. Transfer cookies to racks. Spoon about ½ teaspoon jelly into center indentation of warm cookies. Cool completely on racks. Store in an airtight container at room temperature 1 week; freeze for longer storage.

2½ cups all-purpose flour
2 teaspoons baking soda
¼ teaspoon salt
1 cup shortening (or ½ cup each shortening and butter)
1¼ cups chunky peanut butter
1¼ cups packed brown sugar
¾ cup granulated sugar
1½ teaspoons vanilla extract
2 eggs
about ⅔ cup your favorite jelly, stirred until smooth

Makes about 6 dozen cookies

Variations

Peanut Butter 'n Jelly Sandwiches: On a lightly floured surface, roll dough out into a rough circle ⅜- to ¼-inch thick. Cut out dough using a floured 2-inch round cutter. Gather and reroll dough scraps. Arrange cutouts, 1 inch apart, on prepared baking sheets. Bake 8 to 11 minutes; cool on racks. Spread the bottom of 1 baked cookie with a thin layer of jam; top with a second cookie to form a sandwich. Makes about 4 dozen cookie sandwiches.

Peanut Butter 'n Chocolate Sandwiches: Form and bake as for Peanut Butter 'n Jelly Sandwiches. Use the following filling: In a medium saucepan, melt 3 ounces unsweetened chocolate, 5 tablespoons butter and 3 tablespoons milk; stir until smooth. Remove from heat. Stir in 3 to 3½ cups powdered sugar to make a thick, creamy filling.

Double Peanut-Chocolate Chip Cookies: Omit salt and jelly. Stir 1 cup semisweet chocolate chips and 1 cup finely chopped salted peanuts into final dough. Roll into balls as directed; use a fork to flatten and form a criss-cross on each dough mound (do not make indentation).

Peanut Butter Honeys: Substitute ¼ cup honey for 1 of the eggs. Omit jelly. Roll dough into balls as directed; use a fork to flatten and form a criss-cross on each dough mound (do not make indentation). Before baking, drizzle top of each cookie with about ¼ teaspoon honey.

(continued on page 134)

Peanut-Chocolate Kiss Cookies: You will need about 72 foil-wrapped milk chocolate kiss candies. Omit jelly. Roll dough into balls as directed; roll balls in granulated sugar. Bake 6 minutes. Remove from oven and place an unwrapped chocolate candy, pointed side up, on center top of each cookie. Gently but firmly press candy down about ⅜ inch into cookie. Return to oven and bake an additional 5 to 7 minutes.

Peanut Butter-Orange Cookies: Omit jelly. Add the finely grated zest of 1 large orange to shortening mixture before beating. Roll dough into balls as directed; use a fork to flatten and form a criss-cross on each dough mound (do not make indentation). Bake and cool as directed. Drizzle cooled cookies with the following glaze: In a medium bowl, combine 2 cups powdered sugar (sifted), 1 teaspoon vanilla and 2 to 4 tablespoons orange juice. Glaze should be smooth, creamy and a medium consistency.

Peanut Butter-Candy Cookies: Omit jelly. Stir 1 cup multi-colored candy-coated chocolate candies into final dough. Drop by table-spoons; flatten slightly with your fingers or the back of a spoon.

Pigtails

(Kosichki, from Russia)

Called "pigtails" because the dough is braided, these cookies are both delicious and beautiful. A quick tip when braiding any kind of dough is to work from the middle toward each end to create a more uniform braid. This dough is rich with sour cream and is really more like a pastry than a cookie.

1 In a medium bowl, combine flour, ¼ cup poppy seed and baking soda; set aside. In a large mixing bowl, beat butter, sugar and salt together until combined. Add eggs one at a time, beating well after each addition. Beat in sour cream and vanilla. Add flour mixture, 1 cup at a time, stirring well after each addition. Gather dough into a ball. Wrap in waxed paper or plastic wrap; and refrigerate 1 hour.

2 Preheat oven to 375°F. Lightly grease 2 large baking sheets. Divide dough in half; refrigerate one half. On a well-floured surface, roll out half of dough to a 15- x 5-inch rectangle, ¼ inch thick. Using a floured knife, cut dough into 60 (5- x ¼-inch) strips; dip knife in flour often to facilitate cutting.

3 Lay 3 strips of dough side by side on floured work surface. Braid strips; pinch ends together. Brush completed braids with egg white glaze; sprinkle lightly with additional poppy seed. Arrange braids, 1 inch apart, on prepared baking sheets. Repeat with second half of dough.

4 Bake 13 to 16 minutes, or until golden and crisp. Cool on racks. Store in an airtight container at room temperature 5 days; freeze for longer storage.

3 cups all-purpose flour
¼ cup poppy seed
½ teaspoon baking soda
½ cup butter, softened
1 cup granulated sugar
½ teaspoon salt
2 eggs
½ cup sour cream
1 teaspoon vanilla extract
1 egg white beaten with 2 teaspoons water for glaze
about 3½ tablespoons additional poppy seed

Makes about 3 dozen cookies

Pistachio-Jam Cookies

(Karithata, from Greece)

Toasted pistachio nuts give this honey-scented cookie its special flavor. The baked cookie has a jam-filled center indentation. I like the flavor of orange marmalade with the pistachios, but a dark jam—such as seedless red raspberry or blackberry—makes a more interesting visual contrast. If you can find it, rose petal jam makes a delicious filling that will intrigue your tastebuds.

1 In a large mixing bowl, beat butter, sugar, honey, vanilla and salt until light and fluffy. Add flour ½ cup at a time, stirring well after each addition. Stir in nuts. Cover dough and refrigerate 1 hour, or until firm enough to roll.

2 Preheat oven to 350°F. Grease 3 to 4 large baking sheets. Use your hands to roll rounded teaspoons of dough into 1-inch balls. Arrange, 1 inch apart, on prepared baking sheets. With your little finger, make a deep indentation, almost to the baking sheet, in the center of each ball. If necessary, flour your finger to keep it from sticking to dough.

3 Bake cookies 8 to 11 minutes, or until golden brown. Cool on racks. Spoon jam into indentations of cooled cookies. Lightly sprinkle jam with ground pistachios. Store cookies in an airtight container at room temperature 1 week; freeze for longer storage.

1 cup butter, softened

½ cup granulated sugar

¼ cup honey

1 teaspoon vanilla extract

¼ teaspoon salt

2½ cups all-purpose flour

1 cup finely chopped toasted pistachio nuts

about ¾ cup thick jam

2 to 3 tablespoons ground pistachio nuts for topping

Makes about 6 dozen cookies

Puerto Rican Rum Cookies

Unlike most other liquors, rum is distilled from fermented sugar cane juice or molasses, making it a compatible addition to many desserts. Dark rum will give these cookies a more robust flavor, but light rum can easily be substituted. Glazing the cookies while they're hot gives them a beautiful, shiny finish.

1 Preheat oven to 375°F. Grease 2 to 3 large baking sheets. In a small mixing bowl, beat shortening, sugar, salt and nutmeg until light and fluffy. Slowly beat in rum. Stir in flour ½ cup at a time, blending well after each addition. Form dough into a ball; let rest 5 minutes. With floured hands, roll teaspoons of dough into 1-inch balls. Arrange, 1 inch apart, on prepared baking sheets.

2 Bake 9 to 12 minutes, or just until golden on the bottom; cookies should not brown.

3 While cookies are baking, prepare glaze: In a small bowl, combine powdered sugar and milk. Add enough rum to create a thin, creamy glaze. Drizzle glaze over hot cookies while still on baking sheets. Transfer cookies to racks to cool. Store in an airtight container at room temperature 1 week; freeze for longer storage.

¾ cup vegetable shortening, softened

¾ cup granulated sugar

⅛ teaspoon salt

½ teaspoon ground nutmeg

¼ cup dark rum

1¾ cups all-purpose flour

Rum Glaze

½ cup powdered sugar

1½ teaspoons milk

1½ to 3 teaspoons dark rum

Makes about 3½ dozen cookies

Mint Cookies

(Miatniye Prianiki, *from Russia)*

Mint is not used often in Russian cooking, so this cookie is considered very special. The original recipe, dating back over 100 years, called for oil of peppermint. I've adapted it to use more readily available peppermint extract. These tiny, hard cookies are light and refreshing . . . the perfect accompaniment to a samovar of hot tea.

1 In a small saucepan, combine sugar, water and butter. Bring to a boil over medium heat; cook 5 minutes. Remove from heat and cool to room temperature. Stir in peppermint extract and egg.

2 Preheat oven to 350°F. Grease 3 large baking sheets. In a large bowl, combine flour, baking soda and salt. Stir in sugar syrup mixture. (Dough will be very sticky.) With floured hands, roll teaspoons of dough into 1-inch balls. Arrange, 1 inch apart, on prepared baking sheets. Use a decorative cookie stamp or the bottom of a glass to flatten balls slightly.

3 Bake 7 to 9 minutes, or just until cookies are faintly golden.

4 While cookies are baking, prepare glaze: In a small bowl, combine powdered sugar, peppermint extract and enough milk to create a thin, creamy glaze. Drizzle glaze over hot cookies while still on baking sheets. Transfer cookies to racks to cool. Store in an airtight container at room temperature 5 days; freeze for longer storage.

1¼ cups sugar

½ cup water

3 tablespoons butter

½ teaspoon peppermint extract

1 egg, slightly beaten

3 cups all-purpose flour

½ teaspoon baking soda

⅛ teaspoon salt

Mint Glaze

1 cup powdered sugar

⅛ teaspoon peppermint extract

2 to 4 tablespoons milk

Makes about 5 dozen cookies

Raisin Rusks

(Iziumnye Sukhariki, from Russia)

These crunchy, toast-like cookies remind me of Italian biscotti d'anici *because they're twice-baked. Orange zest makes a lovely substitute for the lemon zest.*

1 Preheat oven to 325°F. Grease a large baking sheet. Place ¾ cup raisins and ½ cup flour in a food processor fitted with the metal blade and process in pulses until raisins are coarsely ground. Or place raisins and flour on cutting board and chop with a large knife.

2 In a large mixing bowl, stir together chopped raisins and flour with remaining 2½ cups flour, baking powder and salt; set aside. In a large mixing bowl, beat butter and sugar together until light. Add eggs one at a time, beating well after each addition. Stir in lemon zest and remaining ½ cup whole raisins. Add flour mixture a cup at a time, stirring well after each addition. Stir in almonds.

3 Turn dough out onto a floured surface. Divide in half. Shape each half into a log about 10 inches long and 2 inches in diameter. Stagger logs, 3 inches apart, on prepared baking sheet. Use your palms to slightly flatten logs to a height of 1 inch.

4 Bake 25 minutes, or until golden. Remove from oven; let stand on baking sheet 30 minutes. Reduce oven heat to 250°F. Lightly grease a second baking sheet.

5 Carefully transfer cookie rolls from baking sheet to cutting board. Using a serrated knife, cut rolls at a 45-degree angle into ½-inch slices. Arrange slices, cut side down, on baking sheets.

6 Return to oven and bake 30 minutes. Turn cookies over and bake an additional 30 minutes. Cool on racks. Store in an airtight container at room temperature 10 days.

1¼ cups golden raisins
3 cups all-purpose flour
1 tablespoon baking powder
½ teaspoon salt
½ cup butter, softened
¾ cup granulated sugar
2 eggs
finely grated zest of 1 large lemon
½ cup chopped almonds

Makes about 3½ dozen cookies

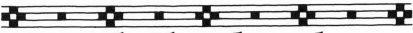

Scottish Shortbread

Shortbread, traditionally associated with Christmas and Hogmanay (New Year's Eve), is now a year-round favorite. The classic large round shape comes from the ancient Yule Bannock, which was notched around the edges to signify the sun's rays. This recipe, compliments of my great-grandmother Kirk, is almost half butter so it goes without saying that it should be the very best unsalted butter available. This is one case where I must admonish, "Please, no substitutions!"

1 In a large mixing bowl, beat butter, powdered sugar, vanilla, salt and orange zest until light. Fold in cornstarch, then flour, ½ cup at a time, blending well after each addition. Dough will be extremely soft. Spoon dough onto the center of a 16-inch length of plastic wrap. Fold long sides of plastic over dough. With palms, roll wrapped dough to form a log about 14 inches long and 1½ inches in diameter. Twist ends of plastic wrap to seal. Refrigerate or freeze until firm, 1 to 4 hours.

2 *Or, to make large shortbread rounds:* Before refrigerating, divide dough into 3 equal portions. Press each third evenly over bottom of a lightly buttered 8-inch pie pan. You can also form dough into 3 6- to 7-inch circles on lightly buttered baking sheets (2 on 1 sheet, 1 on the other). Refrigerate 1 hour. Score each circle into 8 wedges. Using the tines of a fork, prick the circles all over at ¾-inch intervals. If desired, notch the edges of each circle with 1-inch-long slits, ¼ inch apart.

3 Preheat oven to 300°F. Remove dough logs from refrigerator; unwrap. Cut chilled dough into ¼-inch slices. Arrange, 1 inch apart, on *ungreased* baking sheets. *If making large shortbread rounds*, remove them from the refrigerator 5 minutes before baking.

(continued on page 141)

---

1 cup unsalted butter, softened

½ cup powdered sugar

1 teaspoon vanilla extract

¼ teaspoon salt

1 teaspoon grated orange zest, optional

⅓ cup cornstarch

1⅔ cups all-purpose flour

Makes about 5 dozen 1½-inch or 3 6- to 7-inch cookies

Opposite: German Chocolate Pretzels (page 167).
Page following: Spicy Cocoa Thins (page 175).

4 Bake 15 to 20 minutes (a few minutes longer may be necessary for the large rounds), or until pale golden. Cookies are very fragile. Use a metal spatula to carefully remove individual cookies from the baking sheets; cool on racks. Cool large rounds in pans or on baking sheets. Store in an airtight container at room temperature 1 week; freeze for longer storage.

Variations

Nutty Shortbread: Add ¾ cup ground toasted almonds, pecans, walnuts or hazelnuts with flour. If desired, sprinkle top of unbaked shortbread with chopped nuts; press lightly onto surface.

Chocolate Shortbread: Increase powdered sugar to 1 cup. Substitute ½ cup unsweetened cocoa powder, preferably Dutch process, for ⅓ cup flour. *For Spiced Chocolate Shortbread,* add ½ teaspoon each ground cinnamon and ground nutmeg to dry ingredients.

Spicy Shortbread: Add 1 teaspoon ground cinnamon and ½ teaspoon each ground nutmeg and ground allspice with flour.

Chocolate-Dipped Shortbread: Melt 6 ounces semisweet chocolate with 2 teaspoons vegetable oil; cool until warm. Dip each cookie halfway into melted chocolate. Place dipped cookies on a waxed paper-lined baking sheet; refrigerate until chocolate is set.

Shortbread Sandwiches: Spread about ½ teaspoon seedless raspberry (or your favorite) jam on the bottom of one shortbread cookie. Top with second cookie. If desired, dip sandwiches halfway into melted semisweet chocolate.

Opposite: White Chocolate-Almond Macaroons
    (page 178).
Page preceding: Triple Chocolate Drops
    (page 176).

Sesame-Anise Melts

(Galletas de Ajonjolí y Anís, *from Mexico*)

These cookies literally melt on your tongue, leaving the toasty crunch of the sesame seed coating in their wake. They're a bit dangerous because they're not terribly sweet and, before you know it, more are missing from the plate than should be . . . and you're the only one in the room!

1 Preheat oven to 400°F. Grease 4 large baking sheets. In a medium bowl, combine flour and baking soda; set aside. In a large mixing bowl, beat lard, sugar, anise seed and salt until light and fluffy. Beat in egg. Stir in flour mixture ½ cup at a time, blending well after each addition.

2 Place sesame seed in a medium bowl. Divide dough in quarters; return all but one portion to refrigerator. With floured hands, roll rounded teaspoons of dough into 1-inch balls. Roll in sesame seed, coating all sides. Arrange balls, 1½ inches apart, on prepared baking sheets. Use the bottom of a glass to flatten balls to about a ¼-inch thickness. Repeat with remaining dough.

3 Bake 6 to 9 minutes, or until browned around edges. Cool on racks. Store in an airtight container at room temperature 10 days; freeze for longer storage. These cookies are very fragile, so store carefully.

---

2 cups all-purpose flour

¼ teaspoon baking soda

¾ cup lard, softened

¾ cup granulated sugar

1 tablespoon anise seed, crushed

¼ teaspoon salt

1 egg

about 1 cup toasted sesame seed

Makes about 6½ dozen cookies

Kay's "Sneak"erdoodles

(from the United States)

The cookies I remember most fondly from my childhood are my mother's fragrant snickerdoodles, fresh and warm from the oven. It wasn't until I called her to get the recipe for this book that the truth finally came out . . . my beloved snickerdoodles weren't snickerdoodles! It seems my favorite cookie had a rather plain title, so Mom, thinking my sister and I would like them better with a funny name, changed it. They've since been rechristened (by Mom) with the above title. No matter what you call them, they're terrific!

1 In a medium bowl, combine flour, baking soda, cinnamon, ginger, cloves and salt; set aside. In a large mixing bowl, beat shortening and brown sugar until light and fluffy. Beat in egg and molasses. Stir in flour mixture ½ cup at a time, blending well after each addition. Cover and refrigerate 2 hours.

2 Preheat oven to 375°F. Grease 3 large baking sheets. Roll rounded tablespoons of dough into balls. Place granulated sugar in a small bowl. Dip half of each ball in sugar. Arrange balls, 2 inches apart, on prepared baking sheets, sugared side up. Sprinkle each cookie with 2 to 3 drops of cold water.

3 Bake 9 to 12 minutes, or until golden brown. Cool on racks. Store in an airtight container at room temperature 1 week; freeze for longer storage.

Variations

Pecan "Sneak"erdoodles: Stir 1 cup chopped toasted pecans into dough after adding flour.

Ginger "Sneak"erdoodles: Stir 1 tablespoon finely chopped crystallized ginger into dough with flour.

2¼ cups all-purpose flour
2 teaspoons baking soda
1 teaspoon ground cinnamon
1 teaspoon ground ginger
½ teaspoon ground cloves
½ teaspoon salt
¾ cup shortening, softened
1 cup packed brown sugar
1 egg
¼ cup light unsulphured molasses
about 2 tablespoons granulated sugar

Makes about 3 dozen cookies

Spanish Shortbread Cookies

(Polvorones)

These crumbly-rich cookies are of Arab origin, but they're now popular in many versions throughout the world. In Mexico, for instance, nuts are added and they're called Mexican Wedding Cookies. Some polvorones *include lard or shortening, but I prefer the delicate flavor of this butter rendition. The melt-in-your-mouth coating is achieved by rolling the cookies in powdered sugar twice—once when warm and again when cool.*

1 In a medium bowl, combine flour, baking powder and salt; set aside. In a large mixing bowl, beat butter, ⅔ cup powdered sugar and vanilla until light and fluffy. Stir in flour mixture. Cover with plastic wrap and chill 2 to 3 hours or until firm enough to handle.

2 Preheat oven to 325°F. Roll tablespoons of dough into ovals about 2 inches long and ½ inch thick. Arrange, 1 inch apart, on *ungreased* baking sheets.

3 Bake 20 to 26 minutes, or just until golden. Place 1½ cups powdered sugar in a shallow bowl. Gently remove cookies from baking sheets. Roll warm cookies in sugar; place on racks to cool. Roll cookies in sugar again when cool. Store in an airtight container at room temperature 1 week; freeze for longer storage.

Variations
Mexican Wedding Cookies: Stir 2 cups finely chopped toasted pecans or almonds into butter mixture with flour. Roll teaspoons of chilled dough into 1-inch balls. Arrange, 1 inch apart, on

2 cups all-purpose flour
1 teaspoon baking powder
¼ teaspoon salt
1 cup butter, softened
⅔ cup powdered sugar
1 teaspoon vanilla extract
about 1½ cups sifted powdered sugar, for coating

Makes about 2 dozen cookies

ungreased baking sheets. Bake 15 to 20 minutes, or until golden. Roll twice in powdered sugar as directed above. *Makes about 5 dozen cookies.*

Chocolate Mexican Wedding Cookies: Increase powdered sugar to 1 cup. Substitute ½ cup sifted unsweetened cocoa powder for ½ cup flour and 1 cup *miniature* semisweet chocolate chips for 1 cup of the pecans. Form and bake as for Mexican Wedding Cookies. Roll warm cookies once in *granulated* sugar.

Spritz Cookies

(Sprits, *from Sweden*)

These pretty Scandinavian specialties are formed into a variety of fanciful shapes with a cookie press. The dough must be just the right texture in order to press. If it's too stiff it won't push through the cookie press; too soft and it won't hold the design. Stiff dough can be softened with a few drops of milk, and soft dough can be refrigerated until firm enough to press. Almonds are traditional in these cookies, but hazelnuts make a delicious substitute.

1 Place 3 to 4 large *ungreased* baking sheets in refrigerator. In a medium bowl, combine flour, nuts, baking powder and salt; set aside. In a large mixing bowl, beat butter until fluffy. Add sugar 2 tablespoons at a time, beating well after each addition; beat until very light and fluffy. Blend in egg and extract. Stir in flour mixture ½ cup at a time, blending well after each addition.

2 Fill a cookie press with dough according to manufacturer's directions. Select a design plate or tip and attach to press. Press the dough out onto cold baking sheets, arranging cookies about 1½ inches apart. (You may want to practice the technique first by pressing the dough onto a piece of waxed paper.) If desired, sprinkle cookies with colored sugar or silver dragees. If dough becomes too soft, refrigerate until firm enough to hold its shape. Refrigerate cookies on baking sheets for 15 minutes.

3 Preheat oven to 350°F. Bake cookies 8 to 10 minutes, or until bottoms are golden. Cool on racks. Store in an airtight container at room temperature 1 week; freeze for longer storage. These cookies are very fragile, so store carefully.

2¼ cups all-purpose flour
½ cup finely ground blanched almonds
⅛ teaspoon baking powder
¼ teaspoon salt
1 cup butter, softened
1 cup granulated sugar
1 egg
1 teaspoon vanilla or almond extract
colored sugar or silver dragees (optional)

Makes 6 to 7 dozen cookies

Variations

Chocolate Spritz: Substitute ⅓ cup unsweetened cocoa powder for ¼ cup flour; combine with dry ingredients.

Spiced Spritz: Add ½ teaspoon each ground cinnamon, nutmeg and allspice and ¼ teaspoon ground cloves to dry ingredients.

Brown Sugar Spritz: Substitute 1 cup packed brown sugar for granulated sugar.

Lemon Spritz: Add the finely grated zest of 1 large lemon to butter mixture.

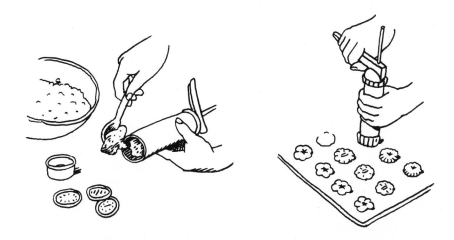

Almond Sighs

(Suspiros de Almendras, *from Spain*)

Suspiros, or "sighs," is the generic name for this popular cookie which the Spanish say is "as light as a sigh." This recipe uses ground toasted almonds, but try substituting ½ cup ground toasted sesame seeds for a delicious change of pace.

1 Preheat oven to 250°F. Grease and flour 3 or 4 large baking sheets. In a medium bowl, thoroughly combine almonds, cornstarch and lemon zest; set aside. In a small mixing bowl, beat egg whites, salt and lemon or lime juice at medium speed until soft peaks form. Increase speed to medium-high; add sugar a tablespoon at a time and continue beating until egg whites are glossy and form very stiff peaks. Beat in cinnamon. Fold in almond mixture.

2 Spoon mixture into a pastry bag fitted with a ½-inch star or plain tip. Pipe into mounds about 1½ inches in diameter, 1 inch apart, on prepared baking sheets. (Or drop mixture by heaping teaspoons.) If desired, sprinkle lightly with chopped almonds.

3 Bake 30 minutes; do not open oven during baking time. Turn oven off and let cookies stand in oven 1¼ hours. Cool on racks. Store in an airtight container at room temperature 10 days.

½ cup ground toasted almonds

1 tablespoon cornstarch, sifted

finely grated zest of ½ small lemon

3 egg whites

¼ teaspoon salt

2 teaspoons lemon or lime juice

¾ cup granulated sugar

¼ teaspoon ground cinnamon

about ⅓ cup finely chopped almonds, optional

Makes about 6 dozen cookies

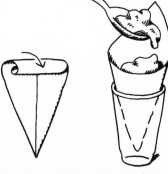

How to make a pastry bag or decorating cone.

CHOCOLATE AND CHOCOLATE CHIP COOKIES

Chocolate's delicious "black magic" has had an almost mysterious hold over human taste buds for centuries. It's been to Elba with Napoleon, to Mount Everest with Hillary and to the moon with Armstrong! The word *chocolate* comes from the Aztec *xocolatl*, meaning "bitter water." Indeed, the unsweetened drink the Aztecs made of pounded cocoa beans and spices was very bitter. But that didn't bother the Aztec king Montezuma, who was so convinced of chocolate's aphrodisiac properties that he drank 50 golden goblets of the liquid a day!

Chocolate comes from the tropical cocoa bean, or *Theobroma* ("food of the gods") *cacao*. After being picked, the beans are dried, roasted and cracked, separating the "nibs" from the shells. The nibs are then crushed to separate the cocoa butter from the resulting thick paste called "chocolate liquor." An average cocoa nib contains 50 percent cocoa butter, a natural vegetable fat. The "liquor" becomes unsweetened chocolate; adding cocoa butter and sugar creates sweetened chocolate. If more cocoa butter is extracted, the ground result is cocoa powder.

The following cookie recipes all contain chocolate in some form or another. Some are flavored throughout with chocolate, while others contain it in the form of chips or swirls. For passionate chocoholics, I created the *Triple Chocolate Drops*—a dark chocolate cookie, full of chocolate chips, crowned with a white chocolate glaze and decorated with more grated chocolate. One of these will send you to chocolate heaven!

Black & White-Chocolate Checkerboards

(from the United States)

These cookies are definitely an "event." Strips of dark and white chocolate dough are formed to create a square checkerboard cookie that's almost too beautiful to eat! As with any special creation, this one takes time, but the showstopping results are definitely worth the effort. Because they're so unique, Black & White Checkerboards make a lovely and loving gift for someone special.

1 In a large mixing bowl, beat butter, sugar, vanilla and salt until light and fluffy. Beat in egg. Stir in flour ½ cup at a time, blending well after each addition. Divide dough in half. Blend melted semisweet chocolate and instant coffee powder into one half, melted white chocolate into the other half. Wrap each half in plastic wrap and refrigerate 1 hour.

2 Cut off ⅓ of both light and dark doughs; rewrap and refrigerate. On a lightly floured work surface, roll remaining ⅔ of the light dough into a ½-inch-thick rectangle 4½ inches wide and about 5½ inches long. Cut rectangle into 9 (½- x ½-inch) strips, about 5½ inches long. Repeat rolling and cutting with ⅔ of dark dough. You will now have 9 strips each of the light and dark chocolate doughs. *Do not roll out final third of each dough.*

3 *To assemble the checkerboards*: Place a 10-inch length of plastic wrap on work surface. Lay 3 dough strips on plastic wrap, parallel and touching each other, alternating dark and light doughs. Lightly brush top of strips with egg glaze. Create a second layer on top of the first, placing a light strip on top of a dark strip, and a dark

---

¾ cup butter, softened

1 cup granulated sugar

1½ teaspoons vanilla extract

½ teaspoon salt

1 egg

2 cups all-purpose flour

2 ounces unsweetened chocolate, melted and cooled

1 teaspoon instant coffee powder

3 ounces white chocolate, melted and cooled

1 egg white beaten with 2 teaspoons water for glaze

Makes about 3½ dozen cookies

strip on top of a light strip. Brush with egg glaze. Repeat alternating dough strips for a third and final layer. You will now have a square checkerboard log. Press sides and top to compact and smooth log. Fold excess plastic wrap over checkerboard log to seal. Repeat with remaining 9 dough strips to form a second checkerboard log. Place both in freezer 30 minutes.

4 Place each piece of remaining dough between 2 8-inch lengths of waxed paper. Roll each into a rectangle about 6 x 7½ inches and ⅛ inch thick. Remove top layer of waxed paper. If necessary, trim rectangles to even edges. Brush surface of rectangles with egg glaze. Remove checkerboard logs from freezer. Place the one with the most dark chocolate strips lengthwise in the center of the light dough rectangle. Carefully bring one side of dough up over checkerboard, using sheet of waxed paper to lift dough. Press to conform to log; peel back waxed paper. Repeat with second side; trim dough overlap so it doesn't exceed ¼ inch. Press seam to seal; do not seal ends. Repeat with second checkerboard log and dark dough rectangle. Wrap and refrigerate 1 hour.

5 Preheat oven to 325°F. Lightly grease 2 large baking sheets. Remove 1 checkerboard log at a time from refrigerator. Cut into ¼-inch slices. Arrange, 1 inch apart, on prepared baking sheets. Repeat with second log.

6 Bake cookies 15 to 20 minutes, or until golden brown on the bottom. Cool on racks. Store in an airtight container at room temperature 1 week; freeze for longer storage.

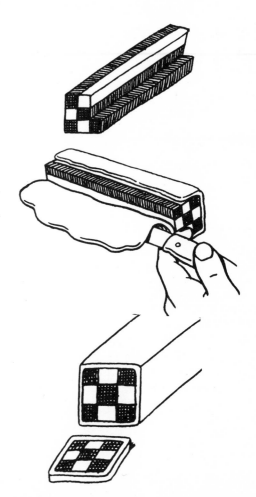

Black Bottom White-Chocolate Bars

(from the United States)

This cookie bar is a delicious paradox . . . it's both light and chewy. A double-chocolate base is topped with a subtle white chocolate layer. . . and finished with a shiny, dark chocolate glaze and toasted almonds. An important tip; the white chocolate should be melted very slowly so it doesn't scorch.

1 Preheat oven to 350°F. Grease a 9- x 13-inch baking pan. In a large mixing bowl, beat butter, sugar, and salt until light and fluffy. Add eggs, one at a time, beating well after each addition. Stir in flour, ½ cup at a time, blending well after each addition. Transfer 2 cups batter to a medium bowl. Stir in melted semisweet chocolate, coffee powder and chocolate chips. Turn into prepared pan; smooth surface. Stir melted white chocolate into remaining batter. Carefully spoon over dark batter; smooth surface.

2 Bake 30 to 35 minutes, or until a toothpick inserted in center *barely* comes out clean; do not overbake. Cool in pan on rack.

3 To prepare Chocolate Glaze: Combine chocolate and cream in a heavy medium saucepan over low heat. Cook, stirring constantly, just until mixture is smooth and creamy. Pour over top of cooled cookie base; use a rubber spatula to spread evenly. Sprinkle with sliced almonds. Chill 15 minutes to set chocolate. Cut into 24 (about 2-inch) squares, cutting 6 strips one way and 4 strips the other way. Store in an airtight container at room temperature 1 week; freeze for longer storage.

---

1 cup + 2 tablespoons butter, softened

1½ cups granulated sugar

½ teaspoon salt

6 eggs

1¾ cups all-purpose flour

3 ounces semisweet chocolate, melted and cooled

2 teaspoons instant coffee powder

½ cup semisweet chocolate chips

6 ounces white chocolate, melted and cooled

Bittersweet Chocolate Glaze

4 ounces semisweet chocolate

3 tablespoons whipping cream

⅓ cup sliced toasted almonds

Makes 2 dozen cookies

Black Forest Bars

(from the United States)

Inspired by a Pillsbury Bake-Off winner, these moist, cake-like bars are studded with cherries and crowned with a shiny chocolate glaze. The one caution on this recipe is not to overwork the glaze. Once you pour it over the cookie base, spread it quickly, then leave it alone. Too much handling and the glaze will turn from beautiful and glossy to drab and lackluster. Of course, it will still taste great!

1 Preheat oven to 350°F. Grease a 10- x 15-inch jelly-roll pan. In a large bowl, combine sugar and cocoa; stir until no lumps remain. Stir in flour, baking powder and salt. Add cherry pie filling, eggs and almond extract and stir just until combined. Turn into prepared pan.

2 Bake 30 to 35 minutes, or until a toothpick inserted in the center comes out clean. Cool in pan on rack.

3 To prepare glaze: In a medium saucepan over medium heat, combine sugar, butter and milk. Cook, stirring constantly, until mixture comes to a boil. Boil 1 minute. Remove from heat. Add chocolate and stir until smooth. Pour over cookie base and spread to smooth surface; do not work glaze too much or it will lose its shine. Let glaze set before cutting into 50 (about 1½- x 2-inch) bars, cutting 5 strips one way and 10 strips the other way. Store in an airtight container at room temperature 1 week; freeze for longer storage.

1¾ cups granulated sugar

⅔ cup unsweetened cocoa powder

2¾ cups all-purpose flour

2 teaspoons baking powder

½ teaspoon salt

1 can (21 ounces) cherry pie filling

2 eggs, slightly beaten

1 teaspoon almond extract

Bittersweet Chocolate Glaze

1¼ cups granulated sugar

6 tablespoons butter

⅓ cup milk

5 ounces unsweetened chocolate, coarsely chopped

Makes about 4 dozen cookies

Chocolate-Caramel Chews

(from the United States)

Absolutely decadent! That's the only way to describe my husband Ron's favorite, which is a combination of cookie and candy. It begins with a brownie-style base topped with gooey-good, nut-laden caramel. Add a drizzle of chocolate glaze and you have a cookie that dreams are made of. One of the especially nice features of this recipe is that the cookie base is quickly mixed in a saucepan without need of bowls and beaters.

1 Preheat oven to 350°F. Grease a 9- x 13-inch baking pan. To prepare cookie base: In a heavy, medium saucepan over low heat, warm chocolate and butter, stirring often, just until melted and smooth. Do not heat mixture any more than necessary. Remove from heat. Add brown sugar and salt; beat by hand until smooth. Stir in vanilla and eggs. Add flour ½ cup at a time, blending well after each addition. Spread evenly in prepared pan.

2 Bake 25 to 30 minutes, or until a toothpick inserted in the center comes out clean. Cool on rack 1 hour.

3 To prepare Caramel Topping: In a heavy, medium saucepan, combine all ingredients except vanilla and nuts. Cook over medium-high heat, stirring occasionally, until mixture reaches 230°F on a candy thermometer or forms a 2-inch thread when dropped from a spoon, about 25 minutes. Immediately remove from heat; stir in vanilla and nuts. Spread hot caramel evenly over cookie base. Let stand until cool.

Cookie Base

4 ounces unsweetened chocolate

¾ cup butter

1¾ cups packed brown sugar

½ teaspoon salt

2 teaspoons vanilla extract

2 eggs, lightly beaten

1½ cups all-purpose flour

Caramel Topping

1⅓ cups packed brown sugar

¾ cup whipping cream

¾ cup light corn syrup

⅓ cup butter

⅛ teaspoon salt

2 teaspoons vanilla extract

1½ cups chopped toasted walnuts or pecans

Bittersweet Chocolate Glaze

2 ounces semisweet chocolate, coarsely chopped

1 tablespoon whipping cream

1 teaspoon vanilla extract

Makes 4½ dozen cookies

4 To prepare Bittersweet Chocolate glaze: In a small saucepan, combine chocolate and cream. Warm over low heat, stirring constantly, until chocolate is melted and smooth. Remove from heat; stir in vanilla. Drizzle over caramel in a lacy pattern. Or pour melted chocolate into a waxed paper pastry cone; pipe over caramel.

5 Let chocolate set before cutting into 54 (about 1- x 2-inch) bars, cutting 9 strips one way and 6 strips the other way. Store in an airtight container at room temperature 10 days; freeze for longer storage.

Chocolate-Mint Cookie Sandwiches

(from the United States)

Two crisp chocolate cookies sandwich a creamy mint filling to create a delicious dessert special enough for your favorite company. The filling can be tinted pink or green, but I prefer its natural cream color. Dipping this cookie sandwich halfway into dark chocolate gives it an extra-professional finish that will bring you raves!

1 To prepare cookies: In a medium bowl, combine flour, baking powder and salt; set aside. In a large mixing bowl, beat butter, sugar and vanilla until light and fluffy. Add egg, then chocolate, beating well after each addition. Stir in flour mixture ½ cup at a time, blending well after each addition. Divide dough in half. Form each half into a log 9 inches long and about 2 inches in diameter. Wrap in plastic and freeze or refrigerate until firm, 1 to 4 hours.

2 Preheat oven to 350°F. Grease 4 large baking sheets. Cut chilled dough into ¼-inch-thick slices. Arrange, 1 inch apart, on prepared baking sheets. Use a cookie stamp to imprint the tops of half the rounds.

3 Bake 8 to 11 minutes, or until cookies just begin to brown on the bottom. Cool on racks. While cookies are baking, prepare Mint Cream Filling: In a small mixing bowl, combine powdered sugar, butter, mint extract and 2½ tablespoons half & half. Beat at low speed until smooth, adding more half & half if necessary. Mixture should be thick and creamy-smooth. *(continued on page 157)*

Chocolate Cookies

3 cups all-purpose flour

¼ teaspoon baking powder

¼ teaspoon salt

¾ cup butter, softened

1 cup granulated sugar

1 teaspoon vanilla extract

1 egg

3 ounces unsweetened chocolate, melted and cooled

Mint Cream Filling

3 cups powdered sugar

⅔ cup butter, softened

½ teaspoon mint extract

3 to 5 tablespoons half & half or light cream

Chocolate Glaze

6 ounces semisweet chocolate, coarsely chopped

2 tablespoons vegetable oil

Makes 3 dozen sandwich cookies

Opposite: Cherry Sweethearts (page 184).
Page following: Crunchy Almond Strips (page 188).

4 Spread a ⅛- to ¼-inch-thick layer of mint cream filling over bottoms of plain cookie rounds. Top with imprinted rounds to create sandwiches; press down lightly. Refrigerate until filling is firm, about 20 minutes.

5 To prepare glaze: In a small saucepan, combine chocolate and oil. Warm over medium-low heat, stirring occasionally, until mixture is smooth. Pour chocolate into a small deep bowl or a 1-cup glass measure. Line a large baking sheet with waxed paper. Dip half of each cookie sandwich into melted chocolate, shaking off excess. Arrange sandwiches on waxed paper-lined baking sheet; refrigerate until chocolate is set. Store in an airtight container at room temperature 1 week; freeze for longer storage. In hot weather, store in refrigerator.

Opposite: Embossed Anise Cookies (page 186).
Page preceding: Vanilla Wreaths (page 203).

Chocolate Marble Cheesecake Cookies

(from the United States)

These cookie-bars are dedicated to my favorite cheesecake fan, my father Wayne. Crushed Oreo cookies form the base for a cheesecake-style filling with a marble of chocolate running through it. The swirled finish is beautiful, but you may choose to cover it with the optional rich chocolate glaze.

1 Preheat oven to 350°F. Lightly grease a 9- x 13-inch baking pan. In a large bowl, combine cookie crumbs, nuts, cocoa powder and melted butter. Turn into prepared pan and use the back of a large spoon or a rubber spatula to press mixture *firmly* over bottom. Bake 15 minutes. Remove from oven; cool on rack 10 minutes before filling.

2 In a large mixing bowl, beat cream cheese, sugar, cornstarch and salt until light and fluffy. Add eggs one at a time, beating well after each addition. Transfer 1 cup mixture to a medium bowl and stir in melted chocolate. Stir vanilla into remaining cheese mixture.

3 Spread vanilla mixture evenly on cooled cookie base. Drop heaping tablespoons of the chocolate mixture onto vanilla mixture in 9 randomly spaced places. Use back of same spoon to cut through mixtures in a wide zigzag pattern to create a marbled effect; do not marble too much or colors will blend and not contrast. Be careful not to touch crumb base or crumbs will be pulled into the cheese mixture. Lift pan about 2 inches above countertop and set down sharply to even surface of cheese layer. Repeat once or twice, if necessary.

3 cups Oreo or Hydrox cookie crumbs (including the filling)

¾ cup finely chopped toasted pecans or walnuts

2 tablespoons unsweetened cocoa powder

6½ tablespoons butter, melted

2 packages (8-ounces each) cream cheese, softened

1 cup granulated sugar

3 tablespoons cornstarch

¼ teaspoon salt

2 eggs

2 ounces semisweet chocolate, melted and cooled

1¼ teaspoons vanilla extract

Chocolate Glaze (optional)

5 ounces semisweet chocolate, coarsely chopped

2 tablespoons butter

2 tablespoons whipping cream

Makes 2 dozen cookies

4 Bake 20 to 25 minutes, or until firm. Cool in pan on rack. *To prepare optional glaze*: Combine all ingredients in a small saucepan over medium-low heat and cook, stirring often, until glaze is smooth. Cool to room temperature. Pour glaze over cooled cookies; smooth with a rubber spatula. Cool 15 minutes before covering; refrigerate overnight before cutting.

5 Use a sharp, thin-bladed knife to cut 24 (about 2-inch) squares, cutting 6 strips one way and 4 strips the other way. Wipe knife with a paper towel between cuts to prevent getting excess cheese-cake mixture into the glaze. Store airtight *in refrigerator* 5 days. Do not freeze.

Chocolate Chip Hermits

(from the United States)

The fact that Hermits have been around since Colonial times can probably be attributed to their down-home, chewy goodness. It's said that the name "Hermits" was applied because these cookies are even better when hidden away for a couple of days for the flavors to mingle. As an inveterate chocolate lover, I've taken the liberty of adding powdered cocoa and chocolate chips to the classic recipe.

1 Preheat oven to 325°F. Grease 2 large baking sheets. In a medium bowl, combine flour, cocoa, baking powder, baking soda, salt, cinnamon, nutmeg and cloves; set aside. In a large mixing bowl, beat butter and brown sugar together until combined. Add egg, then sour cream, beating well after each addition. Stir in flour mixture ½ a cup at a time, blending well after each addition. Stir in raisins, chocolate chips and nuts. Drop heaping tablespoons of dough, 1 inch apart, on prepared baking sheets.

2 Bake 10 to 15 minutes, or until cookies spring back when lightly pressed with a fingertip; do not overbake. Cool on racks. If desired, lightly dust tops of cookies with powdered sugar. Store in an airtight container at room temperature 10 days; freeze for longer storage. If cookies become dry, place one or two apple wedges in the storage container with them; the cookies will soften within a day.

Variation
Substitute chopped dried apricots or dates for the raisins.

1¾ cups all-purpose flour
2 tablespoons unsweetened cocoa powder
1 teaspoon baking powder
½ teaspoon baking soda
½ teaspoon salt
1 teaspoon ground cinnamon
½ teaspoon ground nutmeg
½ teaspoon ground cloves
½ cup butter, softened
1 cup packed brown sugar
1 egg
⅔ cup sour cream
1 cup raisins
1 cup semisweet chocolate chips
1 cup chopped walnuts
powdered sugar (optional)

Makes about 2½ dozen cookies

Chocolate-Mint Kisses

(from the United States)

I created the mint chocolate chip variation of this airy cookie for my dear nephew Tyler, who favors "non-gooey" desserts. It's important for the melted chocolate in this recipe to be at room temperature because heat will deflate the meringue. Don't worry about incorporating the chocolate so thoroughly that it's all one color; a few streaks add visual interest.

1 Preheat oven to 300°F. Grease 4 large baking sheets. In a large mixing bowl, beat egg whites, cream of tartar and salt at medium speed until soft peaks form. Increase speed to medium-high. Add sugar a tablespoon at a time, beating until egg whites are glossy and form very stiff peaks. Beat in mint extract. Sift flour over meringue mixture and fold in lightly. *Gently* fold in cooled chocolate, then chocolate chips.

2 Spoon mixture into a pastry bag fitted with a plain ½-inch round tip. Pipe mixture into rounds about 1½ inches in diameter, 1 inch apart, onto prepared baking sheets; or, drop by tablespoons, 1 inch apart.

3 Bake 30 minutes, or until light and dry. Cool on racks. Store in an airtight container at room temperature 10 days; freeze for longer storage.

Variation

Mint-Chocolate Chip Kisses: Omit melted chocolate; increase chocolate chips to 1 cup. If desired, add a drop or two of green food coloring with mint extract.

4 egg whites, room temperature
1 teaspoon cream of tartar
½ teaspoon salt
1 cup granulated sugar
10 to 12 drops mint extract
2 tablespoons all-purpose flour
3 ounces unsweetened chocolate, melted and cooled
¾ cup miniature semisweet chocolate chips

Makes about 6½ dozen cookies

Chocolate-Whiskey Drops

(from the United States)

In the old South, the word bourbon (derived from Bourbon County, Kentucky) was synonymous with whiskey. And it's this distinctly American spirit that is used in these heady cookies. For a stronger whiskey flavor, soak the raisins in 1/2 cup bourbon overnight, draining them thoroughly before using. Use the drained liquor in the recipe, adding to it if necessary.

1 Preheat oven to 350°F. Grease 3 large baking sheets. In a medium bowl, combine flour, cocoa, baking soda, baking powder and salt; set aside. In a large mixing bowl, beat butter and brown sugar until light and fluffy. Mix egg and bourbon together. Stir into butter mixture alternately with flour mixture, ⅓ at a time. Stir in raisins and nuts. Drop dough by rounded tablespoons, 1½ inches apart, on prepared baking sheets. Lightly press a nut half in the center of each cookie, or sprinkle lightly with sugar.

2 Bake 7 to 10 minutes, or until surface barely springs back when lightly pressed with a fingertip; the shorter baking time will produce a softer cookie. Cool on racks. Store in an airtight container at room temperature 1 week; freeze for longer storage.

2 cups all-purpose flour
¼ cup unsweetened cocoa powder
1 teaspoon baking soda
½ teaspoon baking powder
½ teaspoon salt
⅔ cup butter, softened
1 cup packed brown sugar
1 egg
⅓ cup + 1 tablespoon bourbon
½ cup raisins
½ cup chopped pecans or walnuts
about 48 pecan or walnut halves, or coarse decorating sugar

Makes about 4 dozen cookies

Bear Paws

(Medvědí Tlapičvky, *from Czechoslovakia*)

This spicy chocolate cookie is traditionally shaped to look like a big brown bear paw. You'll probably have to make your own bear-paw pattern out of cardboard. Lacking that, however, the dough may be rolled out and cut with your favorite cookie cutter, or cut freehand with a pointed knife. I simply use a large teddy bear cooking cutter. The results are equally delicious!

1 Preheat oven to 350°F. Grease 2 large baking sheets. In a medium bowl, combine flour, cocoa and nuts; set aside. In a large mixing bowl, beat butter, sugar, cinnamon, cloves and salt together until combined. Add eggs one at a time, beating well after each addition. Stir in flour mixture a cup at a time, blending well after each addition. Form dough into a ball; let rest 5 minutes.

2 *To roll out cookies*: Divide dough in half. On a floured surface, roll out half the dough into a rough circle ½ inch thick. Cut out dough using a 3-inch cutter. Use a metal spatula to transfer cutouts to prepared baking sheets. Form leftover scraps into a ball; reroll and cut as before. Repeat with second half of dough.

3 Bake 13 to 16 minutes, or until cookies *barely* spring back when lightly pressed with a fingertip. (Cookies will firm as they cool; do not overbake.) Cool on racks. Store in an airtight container at room temperature 5 days; freeze for longer storage.

---

3 cups all-purpose flour

½ cup unsweetened cocoa powder

1 cup ground hazelnuts

1 cup butter, softened

2 cups granulated sugar

¼ teaspoon ground cinnamon

⅛ teaspoon ground cloves

¼ teaspoon salt

2 eggs

Makes about 1½ dozen 3-inch cookies

Double Fudge Brownies

(from the United States)

For chocolate lovers only, these big, thick brownies are dark, rich and chewy. They have over twice the amount of chocolate as the average brownie and, if you want to be naughty, you can add chunks of white chocolate! Plan ahead, because these brownies need to be made a day in advance and allowed to stand overnight in order to be firm enough to cut. If you're short on time, refrigerate the brownies for at least four hours before cutting.

1 Preheat oven to 350°F. Grease a 9- x 13-inch baking pan. In a large mixing bowl, beat butter and sugars together at low speed until combined. Gradually increase speed to medium; beat 1 minute. Add chocolates, vanilla and salt; beat just until combined. Add eggs one at a time, beating well after each addition. Stir in flour ½ cup at a time, blending well after each addition. Stir in 2 cups nuts. Turn into prepared pan, smoothing top. If you're not going to top the brownies with the chocolate glaze, sprinkle surface of batter with remaining ½ cup nuts.

2 Bake 35 to 45 minutes, or until toothpick inserted in center comes out *almost* clean; do not overbake. Cool brownies in pan on rack to room temperature. Cover and let stand 8 hours or overnight before cutting.

3 To prepare glaze: In a small saucepan, combine all glaze ingredients. Cook over medium-low heat, stirring constantly, until sugar dissolves and glaze is smooth. Pour over cooled brownies; smooth with a rubber spatula. If desired, sprinkle with remaining ½ cup nuts. Allow glaze to set before cutting brownies into 24 (about 2-inch) squares, cutting 6 strips one way and 4 strips the other way. Store in an airtight container at room temperature 1 week; freeze for longer storage.

¾ cup butter, softened

1½ cups packed brown sugar

1½ cups granulated sugar

6 ounces unsweetened chocolate, melted and cooled to room temperature

4 ounces semisweet chocolate, melted and cooled to room temperature

1 tablespoon vanilla extract

½ teaspoon salt

5 eggs

1½ cups all-purpose flour

2½ cups chopped walnuts, divided

Shiny Chocolate Glaze

6 ounces semisweet chocolate

¼ cup granulated sugar

¼ cup whipping cream

¼ cup butter

Makes 2 dozen brownies

Variations

Coconut Brownies: Substitute 1 cup flaked coconut for 1 cup of the chopped nuts. Sprinkle top with ½ cup coconut before baking.

Mocha Fudge Brownies: Add 3 tablespoons instant coffee powder to chocolate as it melts; stir to dissolve. Cool to lukewarm before adding to butter mixture.

Chocolate Chunk Brownies: Substitute 8 ounces semisweet or white chocolate, chopped into ⅜-inch chunks, for 1 cup of the chopped nuts.

Spicy Fudge Brownies: Add 2 teaspoons ground cinnamon, 1 teaspoon ground nutmeg and ¼ teaspoon each ground cloves and ground allspice to flour before stirring into chocolate mixture.

Cherry Cordial Brownies: Substitute 1 cup finely chopped maraschino cherries, blotted well on paper towels, for chopped nuts. Spread with Shiny Chocolate Glaze; let glaze almost set. Cut brownies into squares. Place a maraschino cherry half (blotted well on paper towels), cut side down, in the center of each square. Let glaze set completely before serving.

Frosted Mocha Cookies

(from the United States)

*Few flavor combinations are as seductive as coffee and chocolate—also
known as "mocha." Nuts are optional, and hazelnuts make a particularly
appealing combination with mocha. This recipe makes a lot of cookies so I
usually freeze half of them for future enjoyment. Freeze them unglazed, and
bring them to room temperature before glazing.*

1 Preheat oven to 375°F. Grease 4 large baking sheets. In a medium bowl, combine flour, baking soda and salt; set aside.
In a large mixing bowl, beat butter, brown sugar and vanilla until light and fluffy. Gradually beat in melted chocolate, eggs, corn
syrup and coffee liquid, one at a time, beating well after each addition. Stir in flour mixture ½ cup at a time, blending well after
each addition. Drop dough by heaping tablespoons, 2½ inches
apart, on prepared baking sheets.

2 Bake 6 to 9 minutes, or just until the top springs back when
lightly pressed with your fingertip. Cool on racks.

3 To prepare glaze: In a medium saucepan, combine all glaze
ingredients except powdered sugar. Cook over medium-low
heat, stirring constantly, just until mixture is smooth. Remove from
heat; stir in enough powdered sugar to make a thick, smooth
glaze.

4 Spoon glaze over cookies. Let glaze set before storing cookies
in an airtight container at room temperature 5 days.

Variation
Mocha-Nut Cookies: Stir 1½ cups chopped toasted hazelnuts,
pecans or walnuts into final dough.

3 cups all-purpose flour
1 teaspoon baking soda
½ teaspoon salt
¾ cup butter, softened
1 cup packed brown sugar
1 teaspoon vanilla extract
3 ounces unsweetened chocolate, melted and cooled
2 eggs
⅔ cup dark corn syrup
3 tablespoons instant coffee granules dissolved in 1 tablespoon very hot water
Mocha Glaze
2 ounces unsweetened chocolate, coarsely chopped
2 tablespoons butter
⅓ cup milk
2 tablespoons instant coffee granules dissolved in 2 teaspoons very hot water
2½ to 3 cups powdered sugar, sifted

Makes about 8 dozen cookies

Chocolate Pretzels

(Schokoladebrezeln, *from Germany)*

Though these cookies take a little time to form, they're a real showstopper. Accented with touches of coffee and cinnamon, the flavor is rich enough for the most avid chocoholic. To add an authentic touch, coarse crystals of decorating sugar simulate the salt on real pretzels. This special sugar can be found in cake-decorating supply shops and specialty gourmet stores.

1¾ cups all-purpose flour

⅓ cup + 1 tablespoon unsweetened cocoa powder

½ teaspoon salt

½ teaspoon ground cinnamon

¾ cup + 2 tablespoons butter, softened

1 cup granulated sugar

2 teaspoons instant coffee powder

1 egg

1 teaspoon vanilla extract

1 egg white beaten with 2 teaspoons water for glaze

about ¼ cup coarse decorating sugar

Makes about 2½ dozen cookies

1 In a medium bowl, stir together flour, cocoa, salt and cinnamon; set aside. In a small mixing bowl, beat butter, sugar and coffee together until light and fluffy. Blend in egg and vanilla. Stir in flour mixture ½ cup at a time, blending well after each addition. Form dough into a log 11 inches long and 2 inches in diameter. Wrap in waxed paper; refrigerate 1 hour, or until firm.

2 Preheat oven to 350°F. Grease 3 large baking sheets. On a lightly floured surface, cut chilled dough into ⅜-inch-thick slices. Refrigerate half the slices. Using your palms, roll each slice back and forth on work surface into a rope about 14 inches long and ¼ inch in diameter. Shape each rope into a pretzel as illustrated. Using a metal spatula, transfer pretzels to a cutting board or other work surface. Brush pretzels with egg glaze; sprinkle with coarse sugar. (This step is not done on the baking sheets because both the egg and sugar will cause the fragile pretzels to stick.)

3 Bake 8 to 11 minutes, or until firm to the touch. Cool on racks. Store in an airtight container at room temperature 1 week; freeze for longer storage.

Note

If you don't have instant coffee powder, pulverize instant coffe *granules* or crystals in a mortar with pestle or in a small bowl with the back of a spoon.

Hazelnut Meringue Squares

(Sušvenkové Cokoládové Z Dvojího Těvsta, *from Czechoslovakia*)

A rich hazelnut meringue tops a chocolate cookie base to create this unique Czechoslovakian treat. Making meringue is not at all difficult if you know a few basics. The egg whites must be at room temperature in order to achieve their maximum volume. Beat them just until they begin to form soft peaks before beginning to very gradually add the sugar. Then continue beating until the meringue is glossy and forms stiff peaks.

1 Preheat oven to 350°F. Grease a 9- x 13-inch baking pan. To prepare cookie dough: In a medium bowl, combine flour, cocoa and salt; set aside. In a large mixing bowl, beat butter, sugar and vanilla until light and fluffy. Beat in egg yolks. Stir in flour mixture ½ cup at a time, blending well after each addition. Press dough evenly over bottom of prepared pan.

2 To prepare meringue: In a small mixing bowl, beat egg whites and salt at medium speed until soft peaks form. Increase speed to medium-high, add sugar a tablespoon at a time and continue beating until egg whites are glossy and form very stiff peaks. Beat in cinnamon; fold in nuts. Spread meringue over dough. Using a sharp knife dipped in cold water, cut into 24 (about 2¼-inch) squares, cutting 4 strips one way and 6 strips the other way. Wipe knife with a paper towel and dip into water between cuts.

3 Bake 12 to 16 minutes, or until surface is dry to the touch. Cool in pan on rack. Recut cooled cookies, wiping knife with a paper towel between cuts. Store in an airtight container at room temperature 1 week; freeze for longer storage.

Cookie Dough

2 cups all-purpose flour

¼ cup unsweetened cocoa powder

¼ teaspoon salt

¾ cup butter, softened

¾ cup granulated sugar

1 teaspoon vanilla extract

2 egg yolks

Hazelnut Meringue

2 egg whites, room temperature

⅛ teaspoon salt

⅔ cup granulated sugar

⅛ teaspoon ground cinnamon

¾ cup ground toasted hazelnuts

Makes 2 dozen cookies

Mocha–Chocolate Chip Dreams

(from the United States)

If you love coffee . . . if you love the taste of chocolate with coffee . . . if you love light, buttery cookies that melt in your mouth . . . then this cookie is definitely for you! Nuts are optional, but pecans go particularly well with mocha. Toasting the pecans intensifies their flavor. These cookies pack well for gift-giving . . . and the lucky recipients will thank you!

1 Preheat oven to 350°F. Grease 4 large baking sheets. In a medium bowl, combine flour, baking powder, cinnamon and salt; set aside. In a large mixing bowl, beat butter and coffee powder 2 minutes at medium speed. Add sugars and beat until light and fluffy. Stir in flour mixture ½ cup at a time, blending well after each addition. Stir in chocolate chips and nuts, if desired.

2 Place granulated sugar in a small bowl. Use your hands to roll heaping teaspoons of dough into 1-inch balls. Roll balls in sugar to coat evenly. Arrange, 1 inch apart, on prepared baking sheets.

3 Bake cookies 13 to 17 minutes, or until golden brown. Cool on racks. Store in an airtight container at room temperature 1 week; freeze for longer storage.

2½ cups all-purpose flour

½ teaspoon baking powder

¼ teaspoon ground cinnamon

¼ teaspoon salt

1¼ cups butter, softened

2 tablespoons instant coffee powder (not granules)

1 cup powdered sugar

½ cup packed brown sugar

1 12-ounce package (2 cups) semisweet chocolate chips

1 cup chopped pecans (optional)

about ⅓ cup granulated sugar

Makes about 8 dozen cookies

Peanut Butter Fudgies

(from the United States)

I created these for my dad, Wayne Tyler—a long-time fan of peanut butter and chocolate. A layer of peanut butter streusel is the surprise inside these ultra-fudgy bars. A food processor makes quick work of the streusel but there's one caution: don't process the mixture so long that it becomes a solid mass. It should resemble coarse breadcrumbs so it can be easily sprinkled over the brownie base.

1/2 cup all-purpose flour

1/2 cup packed brown sugar

3/4 cup chunky peanut butter

1 recipe Double Fudge Brownies, page 164, with changes noted

Makes 2 dozen brownies

1 Preheat oven to 350°F. Grease a 9- x 13-inch baking pan. In a food processor fitted with the metal blade, blend flour, brown sugar and peanut butter with on/off pulses just until mixture resembles fine crumbs; set aside. Do not process mixture so long that it forms a mass.

2 Prepare Double Fudge Brownie recipe, omitting nuts. Spread half of batter over bottom of pan. Sprinkle evenly with all but 3/4 cup peanut butter mixture. Drop tablespoons of remaining brownie batter over top and spread gently to cover streusel completely. Sprinkle top with remaining 3/4 cup peanut butter mixture. Bake 30 to 40 minutes, or until a toothpick inserted in the center comes out *almost* clean; do not overbake. Cool brownies in pan on rack. Cover and let stand 8 hours or overnight before cutting.

3 Cut into 24 (about 2-inch) squares, cutting 6 strips one way and 4 strips the other way. Store in an airtight container at room temperature 1 week; freeze for longer storage.

Rocky Road Bars

(from the United States)

"Rocky Road" is the American appellation given to a "bumpy" candy composed of chocolate, nuts and marshmallows. This sensational namesake is a fudgy brownie-type base topped with chocolate chips, walnuts and miniature marshmallows. It's a quick and easy cookie mixed in a saucepan. Layering the toppings in the order given is mandatory in order for them to melt together properly.

1 Preheat oven to 350°F. Grease a 9- x 13-inch baking pan. In a heavy medium saucepan over low heat, warm chocolate and butter, stirring often, just until melted and smooth; do not heat mixture any more than necessary. Remove from heat. Add brown sugar and salt; beat by hand until combined. Stir in vanilla and eggs. Add flour ½ cup at a time, blending well after each addition. Stir in nuts. Spread evenly in prepared pan.

2 Bake 20 to 25 minutes, or until a toothpick inserted in the center comes out *almost* clean. While base is baking, tear off a 15-inch length of aluminum foil; set aside. Remove cookie base from oven; leave oven on. Working quickly, sprinkle the chocolate chips and marshmallows in even layers over hot cookie base in the following order: 1 cup chocolate chips, 2 cups marshmallows, 1 cup chocolate chips, 1 cup marshmallows. (The ingredients must be layered in this order to hold together when the cookie is cooled and cut.) Cover pan tightly with foil, protecting your hands with oven mitts. Return pan to oven for 6 minutes.

3 Remove foil-covered pan from oven. Let stand on rack for 20 minutes with foil covering. Remove foil; cool completely in pan on rack. Cut into 24 (about 2-inch) squares, cutting 6 strips one way and 4 strips the other way. Store in an airtight container at room temperature 1 week; freeze for longer storage.

5 ounces unsweetened chocolate

¾ cup butter

2¼ cups packed brown sugar

½ teaspoon salt

2 teaspoons vanilla extract

2 eggs, lightly beaten

1½ cups all-purpose flour

1½ cups chopped toasted walnuts

1 package (12 ounces) semisweet chocolate chips (2 cups)

3 cups miniature marshmallows

Makes 2 dozen cookies

Soft Chocolate Chippers

(from the United States)

These easy chocolate chip cookies are simply sensational! Crisp on the outside and semisoft in the middle, they're guaranteed to please. Chocolate Chippers have three ingredients that make them special: oats and coconut—which add moistness—and unsweetened cocoa, which delivers extra chocolate flavor.

1 Preheat oven to 375°F. Grease 3 to 4 large baking sheets. In a food processor fitted with the metal blade, or in a blender, combine coconut, oats and cocoa. Process to a fine powder; set aside. In a medium bowl, combine flour, baking soda and salt; set aside. In a large mixing bowl, beat butter, brown sugar and vanilla until light and fluffy. Add eggs one at a time, beating well after each addition. Continue beating at low speed while gradually adding coconut-oat mixture ½ cup at a time; beat 1 minute at medium speed after final addition. Stir in flour mixture ½ cup at a time, blending well after each addition. Stir in chocolate chips and nuts. Drop dough by coffee measures (⅛ cup; 2 tablespoons), 2 inches apart, on prepared baking sheets. Use damp fingers or the back of a wet spoon to flatten each mound to between ½ and ¾ inch thick.

2 Bake 7 to 10 minutes, depending on how soft you want the finished cookie. (Seven-minute cookies will be very soft when first removed from the oven and will need gentle handling.) Cookies will firm as they cool. Let cool on racks. Store in an airtight container at room temperature 1 week; freeze for longer storage.

Variation

Orange Chocolate Chippers: Add the finely grated zest of 2 medium oranges with butter before beating.

1 cup flaked coconut
1 cup rolled oats
1 tablespoon unsweetened cocoa powder
2 cups all-purpose flour
1 teaspoon baking soda
½ teaspoon salt
1 cup butter, softened
1½ cups packed brown sugar
2 teaspoons vanilla extract
2 eggs
2 cups semisweet chocolate chips
1½ cups chopped nuts

Makes about 4 dozen cookies

Opposite: German Honey Cakes (page 192). Page following: Egg Cookies (page 191).

Spiced Chocolate Drops

(Gocci di Cioccolata, *from Italy*)

Each time I tested these delightful, chocolaty cookies I became more addicted to them. They're subtly spicy, semisoft and absolutely delicious! You can adjust the spices to suit your personal taste, and an apple wedge in the storage container will make them even softer. The candy confetti, easily found in most supermarkets, gives these cookies a festive flair that's perfect for special occasions.

1 Preheat oven to 350°F. Grease 3 to 4 large baking sheets. In a medium bowl, combine flour, cinnamon, nutmeg, cloves, baking powder, baking soda and salt; set aside. In a large mixing bowl, whisk sugar and cocoa until no lumps remain. Add shortening and beat until light and fluffy. Mix egg and milk together. Stir into shortening mixture alternately with dry ingredients, ⅓ at a time. Drop dough by rounded teaspoons, 1½ inches apart, on prepared baking sheets.

2 Bake 7 to 10 minutes, or until tops spring back when lightly pressed with your fingertip. Cool on racks.

3 To prepare glaze: In a medium bowl, combine powdered sugar, extracts and 2 tablespoons milk. Stir in enough additional milk to make a smooth, creamy glaze of medium consistency. Spoon glaze over a few cooled cookies at a time; sprinkle with candy confetti. (Confetti won't adhere to partially set glaze, so it's important only to do a few at a time.) Allow glaze to set before storing cookies airtight at room temperature 1 week; freeze for longer storage.

2 cups all-purpose flour
1 teaspoon ground cinnamon
½ teaspoon ground nutmeg
½ teaspoon ground cloves
¾ teaspoon baking powder
¾ teaspoon baking soda
½ teaspoon salt
1 cup granulated sugar
⅓ cup unsweetened cocoa
¾ cup shortening, softened
1 egg
¾ cup milk
candy confetti decorations
Glaze
2 cups powdered sugar, sifted
½ teaspoon vanilla extract
¼ teaspoon almond extract
2 to 4 tablespoons milk

Makes about 5 dozen cookies

Opposite: Wine Cookies (page 212).
Page preceding: Little Brown Cakes (page 196).

Spicy Chocolate Meringue Cookies

(Basler Brunsli, *from Switzerland*)

Named for the city of Basel, this unusual Swiss chocolate cookie is spiced with cinnamon, nutmeg and cloves. Although the "dough" is actually meringue, it's rolled out and cut like any other dough. Basler Brunsli are crusty outside, soft and chewy inside . . . scrumptious!

1 Lightly grease 2 large baking sheets. In a medium bowl, stir together grated chocolate, almonds and cocoa; set aside. In a small mixing bowl, beat egg whites and salt at medium speed until soft peaks form. Increase speed to high and add sugar 1 tablespoon at a time, beating until egg whites are glossy and form very stiff peaks. Add cinnamon, nutmeg and cloves; beat 1 minute. Fold meringue, ⅓ at a time, into chocolate mixture. Fold in Kirsch.

2 Sprinkle work surface with about ¼ cup sugar. Turn meringue out onto work surface and spread to about ½-inch thickness with a rubber spatula. Lightly sprinkle surface with additional sugar. Use a lightly floured rolling pin to roll meringue to an even ½-inch thickness. Cut out with a floured 2-inch scalloped or other decorative cutter, reflouring cutter each time you use it. Use a metal spatula to arrange cutouts, 1 inch apart, on prepared baking sheets. Let stand uncovered at room temperature for 4-6 hours to dry.

3 Preheat oven to 300°F. Bake 10 to 14 minutes, or until firm to the touch; *Basler Brunsli* should have a thin crust on the outside but should be soft inside. Cool on racks. Store in an airtight container at room temperature 1 week; freeze for longer storage.

---

4 ounces semisweet chocolate, finely grated

8 ounces blanched almonds, finely ground

2 tablespoons unsweetened cocoa powder

2 egg whites, room temperature

⅛ teaspoon salt

1 cup granulated sugar

1 teaspoon ground cinnamon

¼ teaspoon ground nutmeg

¼ teaspoon ground cloves

1 tablespoon Kirsch

additional granulated sugar

Makes about 2 dozen cookies

174

Spicy Cocoa Thins

(from the United States)

Talk about easy! One of my favorite cookies—because it's both quick and delicious—is this one-bowl, mix-in-minutes winner that's sure to please all who love the marriage of chocolate and spices. Baked the minimum time, they remind me of a spicy, wafer-thin brownie; a few minutes more in the oven and they'll please crisp-cookie fans.

1 Preheat oven to 350°F. Grease a 15- x 10-inch jelly-roll pan. In a medium bowl, stir together sugar and cocoa until all cocoa lumps disappear. Stir in flour, salt, cinnamon, ginger, allspice and nutmeg. Add butter, egg and vanilla; stir until smooth. Pour batter into prepared pan and spread evenly, making sure batter goes into corners. Sprinkle top with nuts.

2 Bake on center oven rack 13 to 15 minutes, or just until firm; reverse position of pan, front to back, halfway through baking to insure even doneness. For crisp cookies, bake 3 to 5 minutes longer; cookie will crisp as it cools. (Watch carefully. Since cookie is so thin, the edges can singe easily.) Cool in pan 3 minutes. With a sharp, pointed knife, cut into 50 (1- x 3-inch) rectangles, cutting 10 strips one way and 5 strips the other way. Cool on racks. Store in an airtight container at room temperature 10 days; freeze for longer storage.

¾ cup granulated sugar

⅓ cup unsweetened cocoa powder

⅓ cup all-purpose flour

¼ teaspoon salt

⅛ teaspoon ground cinnamon

⅛ teaspoon ground ginger

⅛ teaspoon ground allspice

⅛ teaspoon ground nutmeg

½ cup butter, melted

1 egg, lightly beaten

½ teaspoon vanilla extract

½ cup finely chopped walnuts or
   pecans

Makes about 4 dozen cookies

Triple Chocolate Drops

(from the United States)

A creamy white chocolate glaze crowns these small, soft cookies full of dark, chocolately flavor. Touches of cinnamon and coffee add flavor intrigue to this popular favorite. This recipe makes a lot, but the dough keeps beautifully so I freeze half of it for future use. That way I can have fresh cookies in minutes!

1 In a medium bowl, combine flour, baking powder, cinnamon and salt; set aside. In a large mixing bowl, beat butter, sugars, instant coffee and vanilla together until light and fluffy. Add eggs one at a time, beating well after each addition. Beat in melted chocolate. Stir in flour mixture ½ cup at a time, blending well after each addition. Stir in chocolate chips and walnuts, if desired. Cover and freeze or refrigerate until very firm, 1 to 4 hours.

2 Preheat oven to 350°F. Grease 4 large baking sheets. Divide dough into sixths; refrigerate all but one portion. With floured hands, roll slightly rounded teaspoons of dough into 1-inch balls. Arrange, 1 inch apart, on prepared baking sheets. (If you're in a hurry, simply drop dough by rounded teaspoons onto prepared baking sheets.) Repeat with remaining dough, keeping dough you're not working on refrigerated.

3 Bake 7 to 9 minutes, or until barely brown on the bottom. Don't overbake; cookies will seem very soft, but will firm as they cool. Cool cookies on racks. Cool and regrease baking sheets to be reused.

2 cups all-purpose flour

2 teaspoons baking powder

½ teaspoon ground cinnamon

¼ teaspoon salt

¾ cup butter

1 cup packed brown sugar

1 cup granulated sugar

2 tablespoons instant coffee powder (not granules)

2 teaspoons vanilla extract

4 eggs

4 ounces unsweetened chocolate, melted and cooled

6 ounces chocolate chips

1 cup chopped walnuts (optional)

White Chocolate Glaze

1 pound white chocolate

½ cup half & half, light cream or white crème de cacao

about ¼ cup grated semisweet chocolate (optional)

Makes about 10 dozen cookies

4 While cookies are baking, prepare glaze. Combine white chocolate and half & half or crème de cacao in the top of a double boiler. Place over simmering water until chocolate is *almost* melted. Remove top of double boiler from over water; stir chocolate mixture until smooth. Cool glaze 10 to 15 minutes, or until slightly thickened. Spoon about 1 teaspoon glaze onto the top of each cookie; spread with back of spoon. If desired, lightly sprinkle each cookie with grated chocolate. Let glaze set before storing cookies in an airtight container at room temperature 1 week; freeze for longer storage.

White Chocolate–Almond Macaroons

(from the United States)

The delicate flavor of white chocolate adds its special magic to these airy macaroons. White chocolate—usually a mixture of cocoa butter, sugar, milk, lecithin and vanillin—has just a whisper of chocolate flavor. It can't be classified as real chocolate because it doesn't contain chocolate liquor—the thick, dark paste left after the cocoa butter is extracted from the nibs. Because it clumps and scorches when overheated, white chocolate must be melted very slowly.

1 Preheat oven to 325°F. Line 2 large baking sheets with aluminum foil. In a large mixing bowl, beat egg whites and salt at medium speed until soft peaks form. Increase speed to medium-high, add sugar a tablespoon at a time and continue beating until egg whites are glossy and form very stiff peaks. Gently fold in ground almonds and melted chocolate. Spoon into a pastry bag fitted with a ½-inch plain round or star tip. Pipe into rounds about 1½ inches in diameter, 1 inch apart, on prepared baking sheets, or drop batter by tablespoons. Lightly place a whole almond on top of each round. If desired, sprinkle lightly with granulated sugar.

2 Bake 15 to 20 minutes, or until golden on the tips. Slide foil off baking sheets onto racks. Let stand 5 minutes. Gently peel foil away from back of macaroons. Return macaroons to racks to cool. Store in an airtight container at room temperature 2 weeks; freeze for longer storage.

4 egg whites, room temperature

¼ teaspoon salt

1 cup granulated sugar

8 ounces blanched toasted almonds, ground to a fine powder

4 ounces white chocolate, melted and cooled

about 60 whole blanched almonds

additional granulated sugar for topping (optional)

Makes about 5 dozen cookies

Variations

Bittersweet Chocolate–Almond Macaroons: Substitute 3 ounces unsweetened chocolate for 4 ounces white chocolate; increase sugar to 1¼ cups.

Chocolate-Orange Macaroons: Prepare Bittersweet Chocolate–Almond Macaroons; fold in finely grated zest of 2 medium oranges with almonds.

Chocolate-Hazelnut Macaroons: Prepare your choice of either White or Bittersweet Macaroons; substitute ground and whole hazelnuts for the ground and whole almonds.

Chocolate-Date-Nut Bars

(Gorikhivnyk, from the Ukraine)

This recipe was given to me years ago by a dear little lady from Kiev. It has a thin butter-cookie base which, by itself, would be rather uninteresting. But that base is topped with a luscious chocolate-date-almond mixture enfolded in a cinnamon-spiced meringue. The result? Yum-m-m-m!

1 Preheat oven to 350°F. Grease a 9- x 13-inch baking pan. To prepare cookie base: In a large bowl, combine flour, sugar and salt. Add butter and rub into flour mixture with your fingers until mixture resembles fine crumbs. In a small bowl, lightly beat egg and vanilla together; stir into flour mixture. Form dough into a ball and set aside 5 minutes. Firmly pat dough evenly over bottom of prepared pan. Bake 10 to 14 minutes, or until firm but not browned. Let cool 10 minutes before spreading with topping.

2 Reduce oven temperature to 325°F. In a large bowl, combine chocolates, dates and nuts; set aside. In a large mixing bowl, beat egg whites and salt at medium speed until soft peaks form. Increase speed to medium-high and beat in sugar a tablespoon at a time. Add cinnamon and continue beating until egg whites are glossy and form very stiff peaks. Gently fold in chocolate mixture, 1 cup at a time. Spread over partially baked crust.

3 Bake 5 minutes; remove pan from oven. Using a serrated or very sharp pointed knife, lightly score surface of meringue into 24 (about 2- x 2-inch) squares, cutting 6 strips one way and 4 strips the other way (this will prevent excess cracking of meringue when baked cookies are cut). Return to oven; continue baking about 30 minutes, or until meringue is very firm to the touch. Cool in pan on rack. Follow scoring on meringue to cut into squares. Store in an airtight container at room temperature 1 week.

Cookie Base

1¼ cups all-purpose flour
⅓ cup granulated sugar
¼ teaspoon salt
⅓ cup butter, cut into 5 pieces and softened
1 egg
1½ teaspoons vanilla extract

Date-Nut Topping

4 ounces unsweetened chocolate, grated
4 ounces semisweet chocolate, grated
1 cup finely chopped dates
2 cups chopped toasted almonds
5 egg whites, room temperature
¼ teaspoon salt
1 teaspoon ground cinnamon

Makes 2 dozen cookies

HOLIDAY COOKIES

Throughout the ages, cookies have played an important role in holiday customs and celebrations around the world. The *Greek Easter Cookies* (*koulourakia*), for example, are one of the traditional foods used to break the Easter fast. *Haman's Pockets* (also known as *Haman's Hats* and *Hamantaschen*) are the traditional sweets of the festive Jewish holiday, Purim. And, of course, the baking and sharing of Christmas cookies is an age-old custom in many countries throughout the world.

Sharing your baked creations is one of the nicest bonuses of making Christmas or other holiday cookies. Homemade cookies make a wonderfully warm welcome for visitors, the perfect tea accompaniment or a delicious thank-you for teacher, boss or postman. And festively wrapped, beribboned packages of homemade cookies say "you're special" in a way no other gift can. Gather interesting cookie containers (such as old-fashioned crocks, unusual tins and colorful baskets) throughout the year for holiday gift giving. It's a nice touch to include the recipe of the cookies you're giving in your gift package.

The following pages abound with holiday cookies from over 18 countries. There are traditional recipes, like German *Springerle*, American *Moravian Molasses Cookies* and Danish *Vanilla Wreaths*. Others, such as *Pumpkin Halloween Cookies* and *"Stained Glass" Christmas Cookies*, can become a new tradition. Remember, you can never have enough cookies on hand during the holidays . . . so start baking early!

Alsatian Christmas Cookies

(Schwowebredles)

Alsace-Lorraine is a small region in northeast France. Its people are part French and part German, and the Alsatian food reflects the best of both cuisines. Spicy with cinnamon, these buttery-crisp cookies are a favorite during the Christmas season.

1 In a medium bowl, combine flour, almonds, cinnamon and salt; set aside. In a large mixing bowl, beat butter, sugar and vanilla together until light and fluffy. Stir in flour mixture ½ cup at a time, blending well after each addition. Stir in orange peel. Cover dough and refrigerate 2 hours.

2 Preheat oven to 375°F. Grease 3 to 4 large baking sheets. On a floured work surface, roll dough out into a rough circle ¼ inch thick. Cut out dough using floured 2-inch cutters in Christmas shapes. Gather and reroll dough scraps. Brush cutouts with egg glaze; decorate with colored sugar or silver dragees. Arrange 1 inch apart on prepared baking sheets.

3 Bake 9 to 12 minutes, or until golden brown. Cool on racks. Store in an airtight container at room temperature 1 week.

Variation

Glazed Cookies: Bake cookies without decorating; cool on racks. Prepare a glaze by combining 1 cup powdered sugar and 1 teaspoon vanilla extract in a medium bowl. Stir in enough orange juice (1 to 2 tablespoons) to make a smooth, thin glaze. Spoon glaze over cooled cookies; sprinkle with colored sugar.

1⅓ cups all-purpose flour
1 cup ground toasted almonds
2 teaspoons ground cinnamon
¼ teaspoon salt
¾ cup butter, softened
¾ cup granulated sugar
1 teaspoon vanilla extract
¼ cup candied orange peel, minced
1 egg white beaten with 2 teaspoons water for glaze
colored sugar or silver dragees

Makes about 4½ dozen cookies

Butter-Walnut Greeks

(Kourabiedes, *from Greece*)

Probably the most popular Greek cookie, kourabiedes are always served at festive occasions—from christenings to weddings to holiday celebrations. At Christmastime, they're studded with a clove to symbolize the rare spices brought to Christ by the Magi. There are probably as many versions of kourabiedes as there are Greek cooks. Some require walnuts, others almonds, while others omit nuts entirely. They come in all forms—from balls to ovals to S-shapes.

1 In a medium bowl, combine flour, walnuts, baking powder and salt; set aside. In a large mixing bowl, beat butter and sugar until light and fluffy. Add egg yolk, brandy and vanilla, beating well after each addition. Stir in flour mixture, ½ cup at a time, blending well after each addition. Cover bowl with plastic wrap and refrigerate dough 3 to 4 hours, or until firm enough to handle.

2 Preheat oven to 325°F. Grease 4 large baking sheets. Roll rounded teaspoons of dough into 1-inch balls. Insert a whole clove in the top of each ball, if desired. Or, working with rounded tablespoons of dough, use your palms to roll each piece back and forth on a lightly floured work surface until it forms a 5-inch rope. Form into an S-shape. Arrange balls or S-shapes, 1 inch apart, on prepared baking sheets.

3 Bake 13 to 18 minutes, or until barely golden. Place cookies on wire racks. (The S-shaped cookies are very fragile, so handle carefully.) Immediately sift powdered sugar generously over cookies. Cool completely on racks. Store in an airtight container at room temperature 2 weeks; freeze for longer storage.

---

2 cups all-purpose flour
¾ cup ground toasted walnuts
½ teaspoon baking powder
¼ teaspoon salt
1 cup butter, softened
½ cup powdered sugar
1 egg yolk
2 tablespoons brandy
½ teaspoon vanilla extract
about 72 whole cloves, optional
additional powdered sugar

Makes about 6 dozen 1-inch ball-shape
Or 4 dozen S-shaped cookies

Cherry Sweethearts

(from England)

In many English towns, sandwich cookies are referred to as "sweethearts." These examples are cherry cookies sandwiched with cherry jam for a double flavor treat. Because they're so pretty, and the dough can be cut into many shapes, Cherry Sweethearts are perfect for holidays. I make hearts for Valentine's Day, hatchets for Washington's birthday and wreaths for Christmas.

1 In a large mixing bowl, beat butter, sugar and salt until light and fluffy. Add vanilla, then eggs, one at a time, beating well after each addition. Stir in nutmeg, then flour, ½ cup at a time, blending well after each addition. Stir in cherries. Form dough into a ball; wrap and refrigerate 30 minutes.

2 Preheat oven to 350°F. Grease 4 large baking sheets. On a well-floured surface, roll dough out into a rough circle ⅛ inch thick. Cut out dough using a floured 2½-inch scalloped cutter, pressing it down firmly to make sure it cuts through pieces of cherry in dough. Arrange rounds 1 inch apart on prepared baking sheets.

3 Bake 13 to 16 minutes, or until pale golden brown. Cool on racks.

4 Prepare glaze by combining powdered sugar with enough maraschino cherry juice to make a thick, smooth mixture. Spoon a scant teaspoon of glaze over the tops of half of the cookies, spreading to within ½ inch of the edge. Let glaze set 4 to 5 minutes, then place a maraschino cherry half in the center of each glazed cookie. Allow glaze to set completely. Spread a thin layer of cherry jam over bottoms of remaining cookies. Top with glazed cookies, forming a sandwich. Store in an airtight container at room temperature 1 week; freeze for longer storage.

1 cup butter, softened
1 cup granulated sugar
¼ teaspoon salt
1½ teaspoons vanilla extract
2 eggs
½ teaspoon ground nutmeg
3 cups all-purpose flour
⅔ cup finely chopped maraschino cherries, blotted very well on paper towels

Glaze

1½ cups powdered sugar
3 to 4 tablespoons maraschino cherry juice
about 30 maraschino cherries, halved and blotted well on paper towels
about ½ cup cherry jam (finely chop any large pieces of cherry)

Makes about 5 dozen cookies

Cinnamon Stars

(Zimtsterne, from Switzerland)

These traditional holiday cookies are of German origin. Made without flour or butter, Cinnamon Stars are delicate and light. The dough, which is really a nut-laced meringue, is very sticky and somewhat temperamental to work with. Before baking, the cookies are frosted with plain meringue for a swirling, shiny finish.

1 In a small mixing bowl, beat egg whites at medium speed until soft peaks form. Increase speed to high and add sugar 1 tablespoon at a time, beating until egg whites form very stiff, glossy peaks. Set aside 1 cup of the meringue. Beat lemon zest, cinnamon and salt into remaining meringue mixture; fold in almonds.

2 Lightly flour work surface; sprinkle with granulated sugar. Turn meringue out onto work surface and spread about ⅜ inch thick using a rubber spatula. Let stand, uncovered, at room temperature 30 minutes.

3 Preheat oven to 275°F. Grease and flour 3 large baking sheets. Using a lightly floured rolling pin, roll out dough ¼ inch thick. Cut out dough using a floured 1½-inch star-shaped cutter, reflouring cutter with each use. Arrange stars, 1 inch apart, on prepared baking sheets. Reroll and cut scraps. Using a very small pastry brush (a medium artist's brush works best) or the back of a small spoon, carefully paint the top of each cookie with some of the reserved meringue.

4 Bake 14 to 16 minutes, or until surface is firm and dry to the touch. Cool on racks. Store in an airtight container at room temperature 1 week; freeze for longer storage.

3 egg whites, room temperature
2 cups powdered sugar
2 teaspoons very finely grated lemon zest
1 tablespoon ground cinnamon
¼ teaspoon salt
8 ounces blanched almonds, finely ground
about 2 tablespoons granulated sugar

Makes about 5 dozen cookies

185

Embossed Anise Cookies

(Springerle, *from Germany*)

I was introduced to these elegant cookies at a Christmas cookie swap and it was love at first bite! Springerle, one of Germany's most famous Christmas sweets, is a beautifully embossed cookie that originated centuries ago in the German duchy of Swabia. The embossed designs are formed with a special carved rolling pin or wooden mold. The dough is stamped with the design, cut out and then allowed to dry overnight to set the design before the cookies are baked.

1 Grease 4 large baking sheets with softened butter. Sprinkle anise seed evenly over sheets. In a large mixing bowl, beat eggs and salt until light. Beating constantly at medium speed, gradually add sugar ¼ cup at a time, blending well after each addition and scraping bowl as necessary. Increase speed to high; continue beating until mixture is thick and pale and forms ribbons in bowl when beaters are lifted, 5 to 10 minutes. Fold in lemon zest, then flour, ½ cup at a time, blending well after each addition.

2 Turn dough out onto a well-floured surface. Use pastry scraper (or metal spatula) and heels of palms to knead dough 3 minutes, adding flour to work surface as necessary. Do not dig into dough with your fingers. Finished dough should be soft, smooth and pliable.

3 Divide dough in half. Roll each half out into a rectangle about ½ inch thick and slightly wider than your *Springerle* rolling pin. Make sure surface of dough is even or it will not imprint well. Dust *Springerle* pin with flour. Roll pin over dough, pressing down firmly to imprint designs; dough will flatten slightly to about ⅜ inch thick. Using a pastry brush, lightly whisk any excess flour from

softened unsalted butter for baking sheets

¼ cup anise seed

4 eggs

½ teaspoon salt

1 pound powdered sugar

very finely grated zest of 1 medium lemon

3¼ cups all-purpose flour

Makes about 5 dozen 2-inch cookies made with a Springerle rolling pin.
If a cookie mold is used, the number of cookies will depend on the size of the mold.

tops of cookies. Using a floured knife with a long, thin blade, cut designs apart. Arrange, ½ inch apart, on prepared baking sheets. Gather dough scraps into a ball, reroll and cut; dust rolling pin with flour before each imprinting. Let cookies stand for 12 hours, uncovered, at room temperature.

4 *To use Springerle cookie molds*, generously dust molds with flour. Lightly press dough into molds; level off with a sharp knife. Unmold by inverting the mold over the prepared baking sheet and tapping; if necessary, use the tip of a pointed knife to loosen the edge of the dough. Brush excess flour from surface of cookie. Reflour mold before using again.

5 Preheat oven to 300°F. Bake cookies 15 to 20 minutes, or until nearly firm; cookies should not color. Cool on racks. Store in an airtight container at room temperature 1 week before serving. Store airtight 3 to 4 weeks; freeze for longer storage.

Note

Sprinkle any anise seed remaining on baking sheets over bottom of container in which you store the *Springerle*. The seed will perfume the cookies with additional anise fragrance.

Crunchy Almond Strips

(Mazurek Wielkanocny, *from Poland)*

Hard-cooked egg yolks add rich richness to these Polish specialties, which are always served on Easter Sunday. This is the traditional recipe, but I have a Polish friend who spreads her mazurek *with melted chocolate before sprinkling almonds over the surface. Chocolate fans will undoubtedly enjoy Olga's variation, given below.*

1 Preheat oven to 350°. Grease and flour a 10- x 15-inch jelly-roll pan. In a large bowl, combine flour, 1 cup sugar, salt, egg yolks and orange zest. Add butter and extracts. Rub butter into flour mixture with your fingers until well combined. Use your fingers or the back of a wooden spoon to press dough in an even layer over bottom of pan, flouring fingers or spoon lightly if necessary to prevent sticking. Pour beaten egg over dough; spread evenly with the back of a spoon. Sprinkle with almonds. Use the back of a spoon to press almonds lightly into surface of dough. Sprinkle with remaining 2 tablespoons sugar.

2 Bake 35 to 40 minutes, or until golden brown. Cut warm cookies into 60 (1- x 2½-inch) strips, cutting 15 strips one way and 4 strips the other way. Cool on racks. Store in an airtight container at room temperature 1 week; freeze for longer storage.

Variation

Chocolate-Glazed Mazurek: Omit beaten eggs. Melt 3 ounces semisweet chocolate; cool to room temperature. Drizzle melted and cooled chocolate over dough that has been pressed into pan. Spread evenly with the back of a spoon. Sprinkle with almonds and sugar. Bake as usual.

2 cups all-purpose flour
1 cup + 2 tablespoons granulated sugar
¼ teaspoon salt
4 hard-cooked egg yolks, sieved
finely grated zest of 1 small orange
1 cup butter, cut into 16 pieces and softened
1 teaspoon vanilla extract
¼ teaspoon almond extract
1 egg, lightly beaten
1 cup sliced almonds

Makes 5 dozen cookies

Opposite: Moravian Molasses Cookies (page 197).
Page following: Scandinavian Peppernuts (page 209).

Ginger Shamrocks

(from Ireland)

'Tis sure these gingery shamrocks will bring out the Irish in you! Crisp and spicy, these large, round cookies have a sparkling-green shamrock in the center. I use the coarse decorating sugar found in cake-decorating supply shops, because it retains its sparkle better after baking.

1 In a medium bowl, combine flour, ginger, cinnamon, baking soda and salt; set aside. In a large mixing bowl, beat butter, sugar and vanilla together until light and fluffy. Stir in flour mixture ½ cup at a time, blending well after each addition.

2 Divide dough in half. On a floured surface, roll each half out into a rough circle ⅛ inch thick. Cut out dough using a round 3-inch cutter. Gather and reroll dough scraps.

3 Preheat oven to 300°F. Use a metal spatula to transfer slices, 1 inch apart, to 2 or 3 large *ungreased* baking sheets. Lightly place a 2- to 2½-inch shamrock-shaped cookie cutter in the center of one dough round (or cut out a stencil in the form of a shamrock and place over cookie). Sprinkle about 1 teaspoon green-colored sugar inside cookie cutter or stencil pattern. Carefully lift cutter or stencil without disturbing sugar; if sugar scatters when you lift the cutter or pattern, lightly brush away excess with a pastry brush. Repeat with remaining dough rounds. Carefully place baking sheets in oven.

4 Bake cookies 20 to 24 minutes, or until the bottoms are golden; cookies will not color on top. Cool on racks. Store in an airtight container at room temperature 1 week.

2 cups all-purpose flour
1 tablespoon ground ginger
½ teaspoon ground cinnamon
½ teaspoon baking soda
¼ teaspoon salt
¾ cup butter, softened
⅔ cup packed brown sugar
1 teaspoon vanilla extract
about ½ cup green-colored sugar

Makes about 2 dozen cookies

Opposite: Vanilla Crescents (page 211).
Page preceding: "Stained Glass" Christmas Cookies (page 194).

Rye Cookies

(Ruiskakut, *from Finland*)

I know what you're thinking . . . rye flour in a cookie? These delicious, crisp cookies are lightly sweet and the rye flour adds a wonderful nutty nuance. Their shape is also unusual in that each cookie has a small off-center hole cut into it. Ruiskakut *are traditional Finnish Christmas cookies; maybe the hole is there so the cookies can be hung by a ribbon on the Christmas tree.*

1 In a large bowl, combine flours, sugar and salt. Add butter and rub into flour mixture with your fingers until mixture resembles fine crumbs. Stir in milk and vanilla. Form dough into a ball. Wrap and refrigerate 3 hours.

2 Preheat oven to 350°F. Grease 3 to 4 large baking sheets. Divide dough in thirds; return two-thirds to refrigerator. On a well-floured surface, roll dough out into a rough circle ⅛ inch thick. Cut out dough using a floured 2-inch round cutter; do not twist cutter because dough is delicate and tears easily. Use a ½-inch round cutter (the cap from a small bottle of flavoring extract is a little larger, but will work) to cut an off-center hole in each cookie round. If necessary, use the tip of a pointed knife to lift dough out of the hole. Add dough "holes" and other scraps to dough in refrigerator. Repeat rolling and cutting with remaining dough, working with a third of the dough at a time.

3 Arrange cookie rounds, 1 inch apart, on prepared baking sheets. Using a fork, deeply prick top of each cookie 3-4 times.

4 Bake 8 to 10 minutes, or until cookies are lightly brown around the edges. Cool on racks. Store in an airtight container at room temperature 1 week; freeze for longer storage.

¾ cup medium rye flour
¾ cup all-purpose flour
½ cup granulated sugar
¼ teaspoon salt
½ cup butter, cut into 8 pieces and softened
¼ cup milk
1 teaspoon vanilla extract

Makes about 5 dozen cookies

Egg Cookies

(Eier Kringel, *from Iceland*)

Though excellent any time of year, these rich Icelandic cookies are always made during the Christmas holidays. Sieved hard-cooked egg yolks give Eier Kringel *their fine texture. To sieve the egg yolks, simply rub them through a fine strainer with the back of a spoon.*

1 Preheat oven to 375°F. Grease 2 large baking sheets. In a medium bowl, combine flour, cardamom and salt; set aside. In a small mixing bowl, beat butter and egg yolks until smooth. Add sugar and orange zest and beat until light and fluffy. Add brandy 1 tablespoon at a time, beating well after each addition. Stir in flour mixture.

2 On a floured surface, roll dough out into a rough circle ¼ inch thick. Cut out dough using a floured 2½-inch decorative cutter. Arrange cutouts, 1 inch apart, on prepared baking sheets. Brush with egg glaze; decorate with colored sugar, nonpareils or silver dragees. Reroll and cut out scraps.

3 Bake 10 to 13 minutes, or just until pale golden (bottoms of cookies will be golden brown). Cool on racks. Store in an airtight container at room temperature 5 days; freeze for longer storage.

2 cups all-purpose flour
½ teaspoon ground cardamom
¼ teaspoon salt
½ cup butter, softened
4 hard-cooked egg yolks, sieved
⅔ cup granulated sugar
finely grated zest of 1 small orange
3 tablespoons brandy
1 egg white beaten with 2 teaspoons water for glaze
colored sugar, nonpareils (colored sprinkles) or silver dragees

Makes 1½ dozen cookies

German Honey Cakes

(Lebkuchen)

Lebkuchen, *a specialty of Nuremberg, is probably the most popular cookie in Germany. Culinary controversy has raged for centuries over these spicy favorites. Some fanciers swear they should never contain ginger; others say honey should be the only sweetener. Some like them hard . . . others prefer soft . . . and on it goes. I'm adding to the controversy by giving you a choice of two glazes, one almond and one chocolate. One fact about the delicious Lebkuchen is indisputable—they'll keep for months!*

1 In a medium saucepan, combine honey, butter, brown sugar and orange and lemon zests. Cook over medium heat, stirring constantly, just until butter melts and sugar dissolves. Pour into a large bowl; cool to room temperature.

2 In a medium bowl, combine flour, nuts, baking soda, baking powder, salt, spices, and anise seed; set aside. Stir eggs, brandy and candied orange and citron into cooled honey mixture; stir to combine. Stir in flour mixture, ½ cup at a time, blending well after each addition. Divide dough in half. Form each half into a ½-inch-thick rectangle; wrap and refrigerate overnight, or up to 3 days.

3 Preheat oven to 350°F. Grease 4 large baking sheets. Remove half of dough from refrigerator. On a floured surface, roll dough out into a 15- x 9-inch rectangle ¼ inch thick. Cut into 36 (1½- x 2½-inch) rectangles, cutting 6 strips each way. Arrange, 1 inch apart, on prepared baking sheets. Repeat with second half of dough. Alternatively, roll dough out into a rough circle ¼ inch thick. Cut out dough using a floured 2½-inch decorative cutter. Gather and reroll dough scraps with second half of dough. Arrange cutouts, 1 inch apart, on prepared baking sheets.

½ cup honey

¼ cup butter

1¼ cups packed brown sugar

grated zest of 1 medium orange

grated zest of 1 medium lemon

4 cups all-purpose flour

1 cup ground toasted almonds

1 cup chopped toasted almonds

½ teaspoon baking soda

½ teaspoon baking powder

½ teaspoon salt

1 teaspoon ground cinnamon

¾ teaspoon ground ginger

½ teaspoon ground nutmeg

¼ teaspoon ground cloves

½ teaspoon crushed anise seed, optional

2 eggs, lightly beaten

¼ cup brandy, whiskey or milk

¼ cup finely chopped candied orange peel

¼ cup finely chopped candied citron

additional candied cherries, citron or angelica for decorating (optional)

4 Bake 8 to 11 minutes for soft cookies, 15 to 20 minutes for hard cookies. Cool on racks. Prepare either Almond or Chocolate Glaze.

5 *To prepare Almond Glaze*: In a medium bowl, combine powdered sugar, extracts and 3 tablespoons hot milk. Stir in enough additional milk to make a thin, smooth glaze. *To prepare Chocolate Glaze*: In a medium saucepan, combine chocolate, butter and 4 tablespoons milk. Cook over low heat, stirring constantly, until smooth. Remove from heat. Stir in powdered sugar and enough additional milk to make a thin, smooth glaze.

6 Use a pastry brush to brush glaze over tops of cookies. (I like to brush the glaze over the bottom, let it dry, then brush it over the top and sides. This gives the cookies an airtight seal.) If you wish to decorate the tops of the cookies with slices of candied cherries, citron or angelica, brush only a few cookies at a time with glaze; press candied fruit into glaze before it dries. Set cookies on a rack until glaze is set. Store in an airtight container at room temperature up to 2 months; freeze for longer storage.

Almond Glaze

2½ cups powdered sugar, sifted

¼ teaspoon almond extract

½ teaspoon vanilla extract

4 to 6 tablespoons hot milk

Chocolate Glaze

1 ounce unsweetened chocolate, coarsely chopped

1 tablespoon butter

4 to 6 tablespoons milk

2 cups powdered sugar, sifted

Makes about 5 dozen cookies

"Stained Glass" Christmas Cookies

(from the United States)

Crushed hard candy melts to create beautiful crystalline panes of color in these fun-to-make sugar cookies. They make a wonderful family project for a cold winter day. Unlike some other "stained glass" cookies, these are completely and deliciously edible. They also make stunning Christmas tree ornaments, or they can be hung in a window so the light can shine through the candy panes!

1 In a medium bowl, combine flour, baking powder, baking soda and salt; set aside. In a large mixing bowl, beat butter, brown sugar and vanilla together until light and fluffy. With mixer running at medium speed, gradually drizzle in corn syrup. Stir in flour mixture ½ cup at a time, blending well after each addition. Form dough into a ball; cover and set aside 15 minutes.

2 Group the candies by color. Place one color at a time in a plastic bag or between 2 sheets of plastic wrap. Use a hammer to crush candy into about ¼-inch pieces; crushing the candy more finely can cause it to lose its transparency. Place each color of crushed candy into a separate small bowl.

3 Preheat oven to 350°F. Line 3 large baking sheets with aluminum foil. On a lightly floured surface, roll dough out into a rough circle ¼ inch thick. Cut out dough using decorative 2- to 4-inch cutters. Gather and reroll dough scraps. Use tiny cookie or canape cutters, or the tip of a pointed knife, to cut out designs in each cookie; leave at least ¼ inch of dough between small cutouts or cookie will not hold together. Arrange cookies, 1 inch apart, on

2½ cups all-purpose flour
½ teaspoon baking powder
½ teaspoon baking soda
¼ teaspoon salt
¾ cup butter, softened
½ cup packed brown sugar
2 teaspoons vanilla extract
⅓ cup light corn syrup
about 1 pound clear hard candy in different colors
1 egg white beaten with 2 teaspoons water for glaze
silver dragees (optional)

Makes about 3 dozen cookies, depending on size

194

prepared baking sheets. Fill spaces in each cookie with crushed candy just to the surface of the dough; do not overfill. Brush dough surfaces with egg glaze. If desired, decorate with silver dragees.

4 Bake 7 to 10 minutes, or just until candy is melted and bubbly. Cool on baking sheet 20 minutes before peeling foil from back of cookies. If you need to reuse baking sheets, slide cookies on foil off baking sheets; reline sheets with new foil. Store in an airtight container at room temperature 2 weeks; freeze for longer storage. Place a piece of waxed paper between cookie layers.

5 *To make Christmas ornaments*: With a twisting motion, use a toothpick to poke a hole through the top of each cookie. String a gold or clear thread through hole. Hang on tree or in a window.

Little Brown Cakes

(Brune Kager, *from Denmark*)

It wouldn't be Christmas in most Danish homes without plenty of these thin, crisp cookies to tempt family and friends. They're sweetened with a combination of brown sugar, dark corn syrup and a touch of molasses. Molasses lovers may want to substitute it for all of the corn syrup. Chopping the nuts finely is important in order for the dough to roll out thinly—the thinner the dough, the crisper the cookie!

1 In a medium bowl, combine flour, baking powder, baking soda, spices and salt; set aside. In a large mixing bowl, beat butter and brown sugar together until light and fluffy. With mixer running at medium speed, gradually drizzle in corn syrup, then molasses. Stir in flour mixture ½ cup at a time, blending well after each addition. Stir in orange zest and chopped almonds. Form dough into a ball, cover and set aside 15 minutes.

2 Preheat oven to 375°F. Grease 3 to 4 large baking sheets. On a lightly floured surface, roll dough out into a rough circle ⅛ inch thick. Cut out dough using a floured 2-inch round cutter. Gather and reroll dough scraps. Arrange cutouts, 1 inch apart, on prepared baking sheets. Brush with egg glaze. Lightly press a whole almond in the center of each slice. Brush almonds with egg glaze.

3 Bake cookies 7 to 10 minutes, or until deep golden brown. Cool on racks. Store in an airtight container at room temperature 1 week; freeze for longer storage.

2 cups all-purpose flour
½ teaspoon baking powder
½ teaspoon baking soda
¾ teaspoon ground cinnamon
¼ teaspoon ground cloves
¼ teaspoon ground ginger
¼ teaspoon ground nutmeg
¼ teaspoon salt
⅔ cup butter, softened
½ cup packed brown sugar
⅓ cup dark corn syrup
1 tablespoon light unsulphured molasses
grated zest of 1 medium orange
1 cup finely chopped toasted almonds
1 egg white beaten with 2 teaspoons water for glaze
about 60 whole blanched almonds

Makes about 5 dozen cookies

196

Moravian Molasses Cookies

(from the United States)

One of the first Moravian settlements in America was in Old Salem, North Carolina, in 1753. These spicy ginger-molasses cookies were a Moravian Christmas tradition for generations before that . . . and remain so today. The secret in obtaining an ultra-crisp cookie is to .oll the dough as thinly as possible. It's a soft dough, however, so only work with a little at a time, keeping the remainder refrigerated. These cookies keep well and will easily last throughout the holidays!

1 In a medium bowl, combine flour, baking soda, baking powder, spices and salt; set aside. In a large mixing bowl, beat shortening, brown sugar and vanilla until light and fluffy. With mixer running at medium speed, gradually drizzle in molasses. Stir in flour mixture ½ cup at a time, blending well after each addition. Cover dough and refrigerate overnight.

2 Preheat oven to 350°F. Grease 4 large baking sheets. Divide dough into 4 portions. Return all but 1 portion to refrigerator. On a floured surface, roll dough out into a rough circle, ¹⁄₁₆ inch thick. Cut out dough using a floured 2½- or 3-inch cutter. Gather dough scraps; refrigerate. Repeat with remaining portions of dough, rolling combined dough scraps last. Arrange cutouts, 1 inch apart, on prepared baking sheets. Brush with egg glaze; sprinkle lightly with decorating sugar, if desired.

3 Bake 6 to 10 minutes, or until golden brown on the bottom. Cool and regrease baking sheets before reusing. Cool cookies on racks. Store in an airtight container at room temperature 3 weeks; freeze for longer storage.

---

4 cups all-purpose flour

1 teaspoon baking soda

½ teaspoon baking powder

1 teaspoon ground ginger

1 teaspoon ground cinnamon

¾ teaspoon ground cloves

¾ teaspoon ground mace

½ teaspoon salt

1 cup shortening, softened

1 cup packed brown sugar

1 teaspoon vanilla extract

1 cup light unsulphured molasses

1 egg white beaten with 2 teaspoons water for glaze

coarse decorating sugar (optional)

Makes about 9½ dozen cookies

Pumpkin Halloween Cookies

(from the United States)

Don't think you have to reserve these soft, old-fashioned drop cookies for Halloween! They're delicious any time at all, and mix quickly by hand without benefit of electric mixer. It's fun to decorate the tops of these cookies to resemble jack-o'-lantern faces—just make sure the surface of the dough is smooth before you start. I use raisins for the eyes, a nut chunk for the nose and currants for the mouth.

1 Preheat oven to 375°F. Grease 4 large baking sheets. In a medium bowl, combine flour, baking powder, spices and salt; set aside. In a large bowl, combine pumpkin, oil, sugar, corn syrup, vanilla and orange zest; stir until thoroughly blended. Stir in flour mixture ½ cup at a time, blending well after each addition. Stir in raisins and nuts. Drop dough by heaping tablespoons, 1½ inches apart, on prepared baking sheets. If desired, decorate tops of cookies to resemble jack-o'-lantern faces; before decorating, make sure surface of dough is smooth, without nuts or raisins poking through. If cookies are not decorated, they may be glazed after baking.

2 Bake 10 to 14 minutes, or until the surface springs back when lightly pressed with your fingertip. Cool on racks.

3 To prepare glaze: In a medium bowl, combine powdered sugar, vanilla, orange zest and 2 tablespoons orange juice. Stir in enough additional orange juice to make a thick, creamy glaze. Spoon over cookies. Let glaze set before storing cookies in an airtight container at room temperature 2 weeks; freeze for longer storage.

2½ cups all-purpose flour
2½ teaspoons baking powder
1 teaspoon ground cinnamon
¾ teaspoon ground nutmeg
½ teaspoon ground allspice
¼ teaspoon ground cloves
¼ teaspoon ground ginger
¼ teaspoon salt
1 can (16 ounces) pumpkin (2 cups)
½ cup vegetable oil
1 cup granulated sugar
½ cup dark corn syrup
2 teaspoons vanilla extract
grated zest of 1 large orange
1½ cups raisins
1½ cups chopped toasted walnuts
Orange Glaze (optional)
3 cups powdered sugar
1 teaspoon vanilla extract
finely grated zest of 1 large orange
2 to 4 tablespoons orange juice
dried currants and additional raisins and chopped nuts for decoration

Makes about 6 dozen cookies

Yugoslavian Christmas Cookies

(Docci Bojai)

This rich cookie begins with a crunchy, walnut-studded base, topped first with a layer of raspberry jam, then a nut-laced chocolate meringue. The result is a symphony of flavors and textures. You can substitute any flavor of jam—just make sure it's not too chunky.

1 Preheat oven to 350°F. Grease a 15- x 10-inch jelly-roll pan. To prepare cookie base, combine flour, nuts, cinnamon and salt in a medium bowl; set aside. In a large mixing bowl, beat butter, sugar and vanilla together until light and fluffy. Add flour mixture, ½ cup at a time, blending well after each addition. Turn into prepared pan; smooth surface. Evenly spread jam over dough; set aside.

2 To prepare meringue, beat egg whites, salt and cream of tartar in a large mixing bowl at medium speed until soft peaks form. Increase speed to medium-high; add sugar, 1 tablespoon at a time, beating until egg whites form very stiff, glossy peaks. Gently fold in ground nuts, then melted chocolate. Spoon dollops of meringue over jam; spread evenly. Sprinkle meringue with chopped nuts.

3 Bake 5 minutes; remove pan from oven. Using a serrated or very sharp, pointed knife, lightly score surface of meringue into 40 (about 2-inch) squares, cutting 8 strips one way and 5 strips the other way. (This will keep the meringue from cracking excessively when baked cookies are cut.) Continue baking 20 to 30 minutes, or until meringue is firm to the touch. Cool in pan on rack. Following scoring in meringue, cut into squares. Store in an airtight container at room temperature 3 to 4 days; freeze for longer storage.

Cookie Base

2¼ cups all-purpose flour
¾ cup chopped toasted walnuts
½ teaspoon ground cinnamon
¼ teaspoon salt
1 cup butter, softened
¾ cup granulated sugar
1 teaspoon vanilla extract
¾ cup seedless red raspberry jam

Meringue Topping

4 egg whites, room temperature
¼ teaspoon cream of tartar
1 cup granulated sugar
¾ cup ground walnuts
3 ounces unsweetened chocolate, melted and cooled to room temperature
⅓ cup finely chopped walnuts

Makes about 3 dozen cookies

Anise-Rum Rings

(Rosquillas, *from Mexico*)

Rosquillas look and taste a bit like miniature donuts, but the rum-soaked anise seed takes them out of the realm of the ordinary. These fried cookies are crunchy on the outside and tender on the inside . . . an irresistible combination! As with any fried food, it's important that the temperature of the oil be high enough to keep the food from absorbing too much oil, but not so high as to brown the outside before the inside is done. Use a deep-fry thermometer for accurate temperatures.

1 In a small, deep saucepan, bring rum to a simmer. Remove from heat and stir in anise seed. Cover and set aside 2 to 3 hours. Or, combine rum and anise seed in a small microwave-proof bowl; cover with plastic wrap. Microwave at full power for 30 seconds. Let stand 2 to 3 hours.

2 In a large bowl, combine flour, sugar, baking powder and salt. Add in eggs, 3 tablespoons oil, anise seed and rum; stir to combine.

3 With floured palms, roll rounded teaspoons of dough back and forth on a lightly floured work surface into ropes 5½ to 6 inches long and about ⅜ inch in diameter. Shape each rope into a circle. Gently pinch ends together; lightly moisten ends with water, if necessary, so they stick together. Use a metal spatula to transfer rings to a lightly floured baking sheet. Refrigerate 20 minutes.

⅓ cup rum
¼ cup anise seed
2 cups all-purpose flour
⅔ cup granulated sugar
2 teaspoons baking powder
¼ teaspoon salt
2 eggs, lightly beaten
3 tablespoons vegetable oil
vegetable oil for frying
1 to 1½ cups powdered sugar

Makes about 5 dozen cookies

4 Pour vegetable oil into a large, deep saucepan to a depth of 2 inches. Over medium heat, bring oil to 375°F; oil should be hot enough to turn a 1-inch cube of bread golden brown in 50 seconds. Using a slotted spoon, carefully lower dough rings into hot oil. Fry a few at a time, turning once, for 45 to 60 seconds or until golden brown. Drain on paper towels. Cool completely.

5 Place powdered sugar in a small deep bowl. Holding ring by side opposite the seam (seam should be pointing downward), dip half of each cookie in powdered sugar; shake off excess. Store cookies in an airtight container at room temperature 5 days; freeze for longer storage.

Bulgarian Yogurt Cookies

(Masni Kurabii)

These delicate nut balls are a Christmas favorite in Bulgaria. One of the ingredients is yogurt—which some researchers claim contributes to the remarkable longevity of many Bulgarian and Russian people. The yogurt-longevity connection remains controversial, but this cultured milk product definitely lends tenderness to these cookies.

1 Preheat oven to 350°F. Grease 2 or 3 large baking sheets. In a medium bowl, combine flour, nuts, baking soda, cinnamon and salt; set aside. In a large mixing bowl, beat lard or shortening and sugar together until light and fluffy. Beat in yogurt, orange zest and vanilla. Stir in flour mixture ½ cup at a time, blending well after each addition.

2 Roll teaspoons of dough into 1-inch balls. Arrange, 1 inch apart, on prepared baking sheets.

3 Bake 15 to 20 minutes, or until the bottoms are nicely browned. Cool on racks. Roll cooled cookies in powdered sugar. Store in an airtight container at room temperature 1 week; freeze for longer storage.

2⅓ cups all-purpose flour

1 cup ground toasted walnuts

¾ teaspoon baking soda

½ teaspoon ground cinnamon

½ teaspoon salt

⅔ cup lard or shortening, softened

¾ cup granulated sugar

½ cup unflavored yogurt

grated zest of 1 medium orange

1 teaspoon vanilla extract

about ¾ cup powdered sugar for
    topping

Makes about 5 dozen cookies

Vanilla Wreaths

(Vanillekranser, ʃrom Denmark)

These buttery spritz cookies are delicately scented with vanilla and formed into wreaths for Scandinavian Christmas celebrations. Pieces of red and green cherry create a festive decoration and a shiny, vanilla-scented glaze adds the perfect finishing touch.

1 Place 3 to 4 large *ungreased* baking sheets in refrigerator. Prepare Spritz Cookie dough using a total of 1½ teaspoons vanilla. Fit cookie press with star disk or tip. Lightly flour work surface. Press dough onto work surface in long strips; cut strips into 5-inch lengths. Working with one length at a time, place on cold baking sheet; form into a circle with ends touching but not overlapping. Lightly press a red cherry piece at the seam; position a green cherry or pineapple sliver on each side to form leaves. Continue with remaining dough, arranging cookies about 1½ inches apart. Refrigerate dough on baking sheets 15 minutes.

2 While dough is chilling, preheat oven to 350°F. Bake cookies 8 to 10 minutes, or until bottoms are golden.

3 While cookies are baking, prepare glaze. In a medium bowl, combine sugar and vanilla. Add enough cream to make a thin, smooth glaze. Drizzle glaze over hot cookies while still on baking sheets; do not glaze cherry decoration. Transfer cookies to racks to cool. Store in an airtight container at room temperature 1 week; freeze for longer storage. These cookies are very fragile, so store carefully.

1 recipe Spritz Cookie dough, page 146, with changes noted below

additional ½ teaspoon vanilla extract

about 8 maraschino or red candied cherries, cut into 8 pieces each

6 to 8 green candied cherries or green pineapple chunks, cut into thin slivers to resemble leaves

Vanilla Glaze

1 cup powdered sugar

1½ teaspoons vanilla extract

2 to 4 tablespoons whipping cream

Makes about 5 dozen cookies

203

Greek Easter Cookies

(Koulourakia)

These golden, crisp cookies are customarily baked on Holy Thursday, just before Easter Sunday. Greek families break their 40-day fast that Saturday at midnight with several traditional foods including koulourakia. *It's said that the twisted shape of these cookies represents Christ's winding sheet and serves to remind us of the promise of resurrection. Greek Easter Cookies keep a long time—and they're irresistible—so you may want to double this recipe!*

1 Preheat oven to 375°F. Grease 3 large baking sheets. In a medium bowl, combine flour, baking powder and salt; set aside. In a large mixing bowl, beat butter and sugar until light and fluffy. Add egg, brandy and vanilla, beating well after each addition. Stir in flour mixture, ½ cup at a time, blending well after each addition.

2 Working with rounded teaspoons of dough, use your palms to roll each piece back and forth on a lightly floured work surface until it forms a 6-inch rope. Bring ends together to form a hairpin shape; gently twist "hairpin" 2 to 3 times. Lightly pinch ends together. Arrange, 1 inch apart, on prepared baking sheets. Brush with egg glaze; sprinkle with sesame seed.

3 Bake 10 to 13 minutes, or until golden. Cool on racks. Store in an airtight container at room temperature 2 weeks; freeze for longer storage.

2¼ cups all-purpose flour
1¼ teaspoons baking powder
¼ teaspoon salt
½ cup butter, softened
1 cup powdered sugar
1 egg
2 tablespoons brandy or milk
1 teaspoon vanilla extract
1 egg yolk beaten with 1 tablespoon milk for glaze
about 3 tablespoons sesame seed

Makes about 4½ dozen cookies

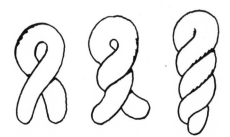

Half-Moon Cookies

(Hálfmanár, from Iceland)

These tender fruit-filled cookies are one of the prettiest in this chapter. Half-manar are traditional Icelandic cookies that are especially popular at Christmastime. They may be filled with fruit preserves or lekvar (prune butter). Though not traditional, I love marmalade in mine. These delicate sweets are best eaten within a day or two.

1 In a medium bowl, combine flour, sugar, baking powder, cardamom and salt. Use a pastry blender or two knives to cut in butter until mixture resembles coarse crumbs, or process in a food processor using pulses. In a small bowl, lightly beat egg yolk and vanilla together. Add to flour mixture and stir to combine. Gather dough into a ball; wrap and set aside at room temperature 15 minutes.

2 Preheat oven to 350°F. Grease 2 to 3 large baking sheets. Divide dough in half; refrigerate one half. On a lightly floured work surface, roll dough out into a rough circle a scant 1/8 inch thick. Cut out dough using a floured 2½-inch scalloped cutter. Place a *scant* 1/4 teaspoon preserves in center of each cookie. Fold top half of dough over preserves so that 1/8 inch of bottom half still shows. Lightly brush filled cookies with egg glaze; sprinkle with decorating sugar. Use a metal spatula to place half-moons, 1 inch apart, on prepared baking sheets.

3 Bake 10 to 13 minutes, or until pale golden brown. Cool on racks. Store in an airtight container at room temperature 2 to 3 days; freeze for longer storage.

1¼ cups all-purpose flour
½ cup powdered sugar
¼ teaspoon baking powder
½ teaspoon ground cardamom
⅛ teaspoon salt
½ cup + 1 tablespoon cold butter, cut into 9 pieces
1 egg yolk
1 teaspoon vanilla extract
about ⅓ cup fruit preserves or lekvar
1 egg white beaten with 2 teaspoons water for glaze
about ⅓ cup coarse decorating sugar

Makes about 3 dozen cookies

Haman's Pockets

(Hamantaschen, *from Israel*)

Hamantaschen are one of the traditional sweets of Purim, the most festive and joyous of the Jewish holidays. The cookies (also called Haman's Hats) are named after Haman, the wicked prime minister of Persia who plotted the extermination of Persian Jews. Haman's plot was foiled at the last minute and the festival of Purim was proclaimed in celebration. Kosher Jews can substitute a non-dairy (parve) margarine if they intend to eat these cookies after a meat meal.

1 To prepare filling: In a medium saucepan, bring 2 cups water to a boil; remove from heat. Stir in poppy seed, cover and set aside to soften 3 hours. Drain thoroughly. Place seed, ½ cup at a time, in a blender jar or food processor fitted with the metal blade and grind finely. Add raisins with final ½ cup of poppy seed, and grind. Turn into a medium saucepan and add orange zest, orange juice, honey, sugar, cinnamon and salt. Bring to a boil, then reduce heat and simmer 5 minutes, stirring often. Remove from heat; rapidly stir in egg. Cool to room temperature. Just before using, stir in nuts.

2 To prepare cookie: In a large mixing bowl, beat butter, sugar, salt and vanilla until light and fluffy. Beat in egg. Alternately stir in flour and orange juice in 3 additions, blending well after each. Divide dough in half. Wrap each half and refrigerate for 1 hour.

3 Preheat oven to 350°F. Grease 2 large baking sheets. Remove half of dough from refrigerator. On a lightly floured surface, roll dough out into a rough circle ⅛ inch thick. Cut out dough using a floured 4-inch round cutter. Gather and reroll dough scraps with second half of dough. Place a rounded tablespoon of filling in

Poppyseed Filling

2 cups water
1 cup poppy seed
⅓ cup raisins
finely grated zest of 1 small orange
½ cup orange juice
¼ cup honey
½ cup granulated sugar
¼ teaspoon ground cinnamon
⅛ teaspoon salt
1 egg, lightly beaten
⅓ cup chopped toasted almonds

Cookie

¾ cup butter, softened
⅔ cup granulated sugar
¼ teaspoon salt
1 teaspoon vanilla extract
1 egg
3 cups all-purpose flour
¼ cup orange juice
1 egg yolk beaten with 1 tablespoon milk for glaze

Makes about 1½ dozen cookies

the center of each circle; spread to about ¾ inch from edges. Dip your finger in cold water and lightly moisten edges of dough. Bring the sides of filled circle up toward the center, forming a three-cornered "hat." Pinch edges of the three corners to seal; some of the filling should show in the center. Brush dough with egg glaze. Use a metal spatula to transfer to prepared baking sheets, 1 inch apart.

4 Bake cookies 15 to 20 minutes, or until golden brown. Cool on racks. Store in an airtight container at room temperature 1 week; freeze for longer storage.

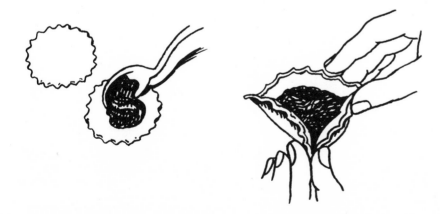

Saint Nicholas Cookies

(Sint Nikolaas Koekjes, *from Holland)*

I am not a spice cookie fan . . . under ordinary circumstances, that is. These extraordinary cookies, however, changed my mind forever. Saint Nicholas Cookies are so rich with butter and sour cream that the dough is a little hard to handle. But their meltingly crisp texture and sweet, spicy flavor more than compensate for that minor handicap.

1 In a medium bowl, combine flour, cinnamon, allspice, nutmeg, cloves, salt and baking soda; set aside. In a large mixing bowl, beat butter and sugar together until light and fluffy. Beat in sour cream. Stir in flour mixture ½ cup at a time, blending well after each addition. Stir in nuts. Form dough into a ball; wrap and refrigerate overnight.

2 Preheat oven to 350°F. Grease 3 to 4 large baking sheets. Roll rounded tablespoons of dough into 1¼-inch balls. Arrange balls, 1½ inches apart, on prepared baking sheets and flatten with the bottom of a glass. Brush with egg glaze; sprinkle with sugar.

3 Bake 9 to 12 minutes, or until golden brown on top and brown around the edges. Cool on racks. Store in an airtight container at room temperature 1 week; freeze for longer storage.

2 cups all-purpose flour
1½ teaspoons ground cinnamon
½ teaspoon ground allspice
½ teaspoon ground nutmeg
¼ teaspoon ground cloves
¼ teaspoon salt
½ teaspoon baking soda
1 cup butter, softened
1 cup granulated sugar
¼ cup sour cream
½ cup finely chopped walnuts
1 egg white beaten with 2 teaspoons water for glaze
coarse decorating sugar

Makes about 4 dozen cookies

Scandinavian Peppernuts

(Pepperkaker, *from Norway*)

It wouldn't be Christmas for most Scandinavians without the appearance of peppernuts. In Norway they're called Pepperkaker, *in Sweden* Pepparnötter, *and in Denmark they're known as* Pebernödder. *Whatever the appelation, there's no arguing the popularity of these nut-size cookies spiced with ginger, cinnamon, cardamom and—you guessed it—pepper! These cookies will keep for a* long *time. I have a friend who swears her German mother kept her* Pfeffernüsse *for a year! This recipe makes a lot, but don't worry; they're addictive!*

1 In a large bowl, combine flour, baking powder, baking soda, pepper, cinnamon, cardamom, ginger and salt; set aside. In a large mixing bowl, beat butter and sugar together until light. Add eggs one at a time, beating well after each addition. Stir in flour mixture ½ cup at a time, blending well after each addition. Stir in almonds, if desired. Form dough into a ball; wrap and refrigerate 24 hours.

2 Preheat oven to 350°F. Roll rounded ½ teaspoons of dough between your palms into ¾-inch balls. Arrange, 1 inch apart, on *ungreased* baking sheets.

3 Bake 11 to 14 minutes, or until golden brown on the bottom. Cool on racks. To mellow flavors, store in an airtight container 3 days before serving. Cookies may be stored, airtight, at room temperature 1 month or longer.

4 cups all-purpose flour
1 teaspoon baking powder
½ teaspoon baking soda
1 teaspoon ground white pepper
1 teaspoon ground cinnamon
½ teaspoon ground cardamom
½ teaspoon ground ginger
¾ teaspoon salt
¾ cup butter, softened
1¼ cups packed brown sugar
2 eggs
¾ cup finely chopped almonds (optional)

Makes about 16 dozen cookies

Swedish Angels

(Anglakakor)

My friend Carol Erickson Henton gave me this cherished heirloom recipe, which has been part of her family's Christmas tradition for generations. The appellation comes from the "heavenly"-light texture of these cookies. The unusual technique of dipping the unbaked dough into water, then sugar creates a crisp topping that resembles winter frost crystals. Swedish Angels are the quintessential sugar cookie!

1 Preheat oven to 350°F. Grease 3 to 4 large baking sheets. In a medium bowl, combine flour, baking soda, cream of tartar and salt; set aside. In a large mixing bowl, beat shortening, butter and sugars until light and fluffy. Beat in egg and vanilla. Stir in flour mixture, ½ cup at a time, blending well after each addition.

2 Place additional ½ cup sugar in a small bowl; fill a second small bowl with cool water. Roll teaspoons of dough into 1-inch balls. Dip tops of balls first into water, then into sugar. Arrange, sugared side up and 1 inch apart, on prepared baking sheets. Use the bottom of a glass or a decorative cookie stamp to flatten balls to about ⅜-inch thickness.

3 Bake 8 to 11 minutes, or until golden. Cool on racks. Store in an airtight container at room temperature 1 week; freeze for longer storage.

2 cups all-purpose flour
1 teaspoon baking soda
1 teaspoon cream of tartar
½ teaspoon salt
½ cup shortening, softened
½ cup butter, softened
½ cup granulated sugar
½ cup packed brown sugar
1 egg
1 teaspoon vanilla extract
about ½ cup additional granulated sugar for topping

Makes about 5 dozen cookies

Vanilla Crescents

(Vanillekipferl, *from Austria*)

According to legend, Viennese bakers fashioned these cookies to represent the crescent on the Turkish flag in celebration of a great Austrian military victory over the Turks. After baking, the warm cookies are rolled in vanilla sugar, cloaking them with a provocative flavor. Vanilla sugar must be made at least a week ahead, so plan accordingly. Though not traditional, these delicacies are just as sensational (and take less time to form) when rolled into balls.

1 In a medium bowl, combine flour, almonds, granulated sugar and salt. Add butter and rub into flour mixture with your fingers until mixture resembles fine crumbs. In a small bowl, lightly mix egg yolks and vanilla. Stir into flour mixture. Form dough into a ball. Cover and set aside at room temperature 15 minutes.

2 Preheat oven to 325°F. Lightly grease 4 large baking sheets. On a lightly floured work surface, roll heaping teaspoons of dough into 4-inch-long ropes. Taper ends of ropes; form into U-shaped crescents. Arrange crescents, 1 inch apart, on prepared baking sheets.

3 Bake 13 to 18 minutes, or until pale golden on the top and golden brown on the bottom. Cool on baking sheets 2 minutes. Place vanilla sugar in a medium bowl. Place 2 or 3 warm crescents into bowl; toss gently to coat with sugar. (Cookies are very fragile, so careful handling is necessary.) Cool cookies on racks. Store in an airtight container at room temperature 10 days; freeze for longer storage.

Ingredients
2½ cups all-purpose flour
1 cup finely ground almonds
⅓ cup granulated sugar
¼ teaspoon salt
1 cup butter, cut into 16 pieces and softened
2 egg yolks
2 teaspoons vanilla extract
1 cup vanilla sugar, page 16

Makes about 5 dozen cookies

Wine Cookies

(Bizcochitos, *from Mexico)*

Mexican holiday tables are always graced by these traditional cookies made with sweet white wine. Lard is the shortening of choice in bizcochitos *because it creates a rich, tender cookie. If you buy fresh lard, it's not at all what one thinks of as "lardy," but tastes and smells a little like walnut oil. If you can't find lard, substitute half vegetable shortening and half unsalted butter. These cookies can be cut into any decorative shape, though the traditional shape of old is said to have been a fleur de lis.*

1 In a medium bowl, combine flour, baking powder, cinnamon, salt and anise seed; set aside. In a large mixing bowl, beat lard and sugar until light and fluffy. Beat in egg. Add wine 2 tablespoons at a time, beating well after each addition. Stir in flour mixture ½ cup at a time, blending well after each addition. Form dough into a ball; wrap and refrigerate 4 hours, or until firm.

2 Preheat oven to 350°F. Grease 4 large baking sheets. On a well-floured surface, roll dough out into a rough circle ¼ inch thick. Cut out dough using a floured 2-inch decorative cutter. Gather and reroll dough scraps. If dough becomes too soft to work with, refrigerate until firm. Sprinkle about ¼ teaspoon sugar-cinnamon mixture over each cutout. Arrange, 1 inch apart, on prepared baking sheets.

3 Bake cookies 11 to 15 minutes, or until golden brown around the edges. Cool on racks. Store in an airtight container at room temperature 10 days; freeze for longer storage.

Ingredients
4 cups all-purpose flour
1 teaspoon baking powder
1 teaspoon ground cinnamon
½ teaspoon salt
2 teaspoons anise seed, crushed
2 cups lard, softened
1 cup granulated sugar
1 egg
¾ cup sweet white wine or orange juice
½ cup granulated sugar mixed with ¾ teaspoon ground cinnamon for topping

Makes about 8 dozen cookies

General Index

Index By Country